High Impact

Rod Ellis
Marc Helgesen
Charles Browne
Greta Gorsuch
Jerome Schwab

Development Editors
Anne McGannon
Michael Rost

Longman

Published by
Pearson Education Asia Pte. Ltd.
317 Alexandra Road
#04-01 IKEA Building
Singapore 159965

and Associated Companies throughout the world.

This book was developed for Pearson Education Asia by Lateral Communications Ltd., USA.
First published 1996
Reprinted 2000

Produced by Pearson Education China Limited, Hong Kong
SWTC/07

Project director: Michael Rost
Developmental editor: Anne McGannon
Project coordinator: Keiko Kimura
Production coordinator: Eric Yau
Text design: Shawver Associates
Cover design: Kotaro Kato, Lori Margulies
Illustrations: Dynamic Duo, Scott Luke, Nikki Middendorf, Amy Wasserman,
            Mark Ziemann, Valerie Randall
Photographs: Don Corning Photograph, The Image Bank, Tony Stone Images
Recording supervisor: David Joslyn

ISBN   Coursebook   962 00 1357 3   Teacher's Manual   962 00 1176 7
        Cassettes   962 00 1172 4   Workbook   962 00 1358 1

Acknowledgements

The authors and editors wish to thank those teachers and students who contributed to this project through interviews, reviews, and piloting reports and provided useful comments for revision. In particular, we wish to thank:

Motofumi Aramaki
Eleanor Barnes
Michael Barnes
Rory Baskin
James Bowers
David Campbell
Torkil Christensen
Cathy Clark
Bill Franke
Jeff Fryckman
Peter Gray
William Green
Su Yup Ha
Hiroko Hagino
Yoko Hakuta
Ken Hartmann
James Heron
Petria Hirabayashi
Robert Hutson

Mario Ibao
Michael Keenan
Chae M. Kim
J. Kim
Chieko Kohno
Koji Konishi
Junko Kurata
Hyuk Jin Lee
Hsien-Chin Liou
Laura MacGregor
Fergus MacKinnon
Peter Minter
Ben Mitsuda
Yoko Morimoto
Hisae Muroi
Ryuji Nakayama
Sean O'Brien
I. Otomo
David Parkinson

David Progosh
B. Hahn Sang
Harumi Sakamoto
Michael Sharpe
Don Simmons
James Stein
Mari Suzuki
Alice Svendson
Laura Swanson
Grant Trew
Charles Tully
Carol Vaughan
Tetsu Watanabe
Rebecca Watts
Robert Weschler
Michael Wu
Yuli Yeh
Robert Zabrovski

We would also like to thank Longman staff for their support of the project and their valuable contributions and advice. In particular, we wish to acknowledge: Dugie Cameron, Jeremy Osborne, Chris Balderston, and Mieko Otaka.

Special thanks to Lesely Koustaff, Shinsuke Suzuki, Kotaro Kato, Marianne Mitten, and Laurie Margulies for their advice during the project.

The authors would also like to express their personal appreciation to family, friends, and colleagues who assisted them during the project, particularly: Yukari Browne, Gerald Couzens, Carl Dustheimer, Yoko Futami, Yoko Hakuta, Brenda Hayashi, Laitha Manual, Michiko Wako, Dale Griffee, John Gorsuch, Georgia Gorsuch, Keith Avins, and Susannah Wakeman.

Thanks to all for your help and support!

Rod Ellis
Marc Helgesen
Charles Browne
Greta Gorsuch   Michael Rost
Jerome Schwab   Anne McGannon

Introduction

Impact is a two-level course to help students develop confidence and skill in using English for communication.

High Impact, the second book in the series, revolves around the lives of four people – Julie, Jordan, Laura, Nick – and their circle of friends. The development of these characters is used as a backdrop for the students to practice information-gathering skills (listening and reading) in context, and as a point of departure for expressing personal opinions about their own lives.

This Coursebook consists of 12 main units and four expansion units. A Teacher's Manual, Classroom Cassettes and Workbook (*High Impact* Workout) accompany this Coursebook and are available separately.

Each of the 12 main units consists of six parts:
Warm Up
Listening
Conversation Topic
Grammar Awareness
Pair Interaction
Read and Respond

WARM UP
This is a short, easy activity that involves all students quickly, introduces them to the theme of the unit and serves as a bridge to the Listening and Conversation Topic sections.

LISTENING
This is a series of three exercises that revolves around a taped conversation. The conversation in this section introduces characters, themes and functions that are carried throughout each unit. There are three types of listening exercises in this section. The first exercise, usually entitled **Listening for key words**, guides students in identifying the key information and how it is expressed. The second exercise, typically entitled **Listening for meaning**, guides students in understanding the main information and central purpose of the conversation. The third exercise is an inference question, **What do you think?**, that encourages students to think about the relationships between the speakers. These three exercises require different but complementary ways of listening.

CONVERSATION TOPIC
This is a guided conversation exercise, based on the topic of the Listening extract. This section helps students develop colloquial vocabulary and learn new conversation patterns and strategies for talking about different personal topics. The section consists of two main stages: vocabulary activation and model conversations.

GRAMMAR AWARENESS

In this section students are required to notice a particular grammar feature in oral input. The first part of this activity is a listening exercise called **Understanding.** Students identify key information about a topic or a character. The second part of this activity, called **Noticing,** is a listening exercise utilizing the same discourse used in Understanding, but with a different focus. Here students attend to the grammatical form, completing a specific task. The third part of this activity, called **Try it,** allows the students to produce and share personal information utilizing the target form. The aim is to raise their awareness of how the form is used in actual discourse.

PAIR INTERACTION

This is a simple pair activity, with two parts. A Pair Interaction is set up first as an **opinion gap activity** so that students will ask and answer focused questions with a clear communicative goal. The second part of the activity, **Follow Up,** builds upon the opinion gap activity and involves a more personalized exchange of information or ideas.

READ AND RESPOND

This section provides reading and writing practice, using a variety of short extracts. Each reading is accompanied by a short task to help focus students' attention on the main information. After the reading activity, there is a short writing task and an opportunity for students to exchange ideas.

After each three units, there is an Expansion Unit. Each Expansion Unit consists of five activities:

GROUP ACTIVITY

This is a structured group activity or short project which extends the topics and themes of the preceding units.

GRAMMAR CHECK

This is a review of the grammar points from the preceding units, utilizing listening or reading input.

VOCABULARY EXPANSION

This is a short exercise that provides expansion of one type of vocabulary item from the previous units.

REVIEW GAME

This is a fluency-oriented activity, such as a board game, that recycles vocabulary and grammar from the preceding units.

LEARNING BETTER

This is an activity designed to raise students' awareness of different learning styles and to allow them an opportunity to think about and plan changes in their own learning styles.

Table of Contents

Meet the characters

Julie Greene

Jordan Greene

Laura Mendez

Nick Koda

David Greene

Lynn Greene

Lian Chen

1 LIFESTYLES

- describing lifestyles
- activities, places
- joining sentences using *and* and *but*; affirmative and negative sentences

Warm Up *My lifestyle*

Look at the activities below. Circle the activities you often do.

drive a car	*watch TV*
travel by train or bus	*study English*
go shopping	*listen to music*
save money	*visit friends*
stay at home	*like peace and quiet*
get home late in the evening	*eat in restaurants*
work hard	*read*
meet friends	*cook*
exercise	*buy new clothes*
go dancing	*write one more:*

Now work with a partner. Look at your partner's book.

Ask questions about three of your partner's activities.

> **Example**
> *What's your favorite restaurant?*

Write the information here.

....

....

....

Listening *"I'm so glad to see you again"*

Julie and Jordan Greene are shopping in the city together. They meet an old friend.

1 Listening for key words

Listen. Check the words and phrases you hear.

- [ ] five months
- [ ] five years

- [ ] boyfriend
- [ ] brother

- [ ] just got a job
- [ ] just graduated

- [ ] buying something
- [ ] just looking around

- [ ] sounds busy
- [ ] not so busy

- [ ] spend a lot of money
- [ ] don't spend a lot of money

2 Listening for meaning

Listen again. Julie has changed in the past five years. Write two things that are different.

before

....

....

now

....

....

3 What do you think?

Do you think Julie likes her new job? Why do you think so?

Conversation Topic *Things I do*

1 Vocabulary preview

Look at the list of places. Where do you spend most of your time? Circle 3 places.
Look at the list of activities. Which do you often do? (Make a ✓)
Which do you never do? (Make an ✗)

Places	Activities
at the office	write a lot of reports
at school	do things with my family
at home	work long hours
at the library	do things outdoors
in the city	play on a sports team
at work	visit friends
outdoors	study a lot
	read books and magazines
your own idea	do volunteer work

2 Conversation building

Read the conversation out loud with a partner.
Change roles and read the conversation again.

Try the conversation again. Use new words from the Vocabulary Preview list.
Now make a new conversation. Use your own ideas.

Grammar Awareness *Two friends*

Jordan and Nick are friends. What do you think they like to do together?

1 Understanding

Read the questions. Then listen to Jordan. He's talking about himself and his friend Nick. If the answer to the question is yes, make a check (✓).

	Jordan	Nick
Does he like jazz?	....	....
Is he interested in movies?	....	....
Does he like hanging around music stores?	....	....
Does he have much money to spend?	....	....
Does he exercise every day?	....	....
Does he like studying?	....	....
Does he get along well with his family?	....	....

2 Noticing

Complete these sentences. Then listen again to check.

1. I really love jazz, and Nick _does too_.
2. I'm crazy about movies, and Nick _____.
3. I love checking out the newest CDs, and Nick _____.
4. Nick doesn't have much money to spend and I _____.
5. I exercise every day, but _____ Nick.
6. I like studying, but Nick _____.
7. I get along really well with my family, but Nick _____.

3 Try it

Write four sentences about you and your best friend.

I _____ and _____ does too.
I _____ and _____ does too.
I _____ but _____ doesn't.
I _____ but _____ doesn't.

Grammar Corner
... and Nick *does too.*   ... but Nick *doesn't.*
... and I *don't either.*   ... *but not* Nick.

Pair Interaction *About you*

1 Choose a topic below. Ask your partner two (or more) questions about it.

Use the question starters or make your own questions.
Then switch roles. Talk about all the topics.

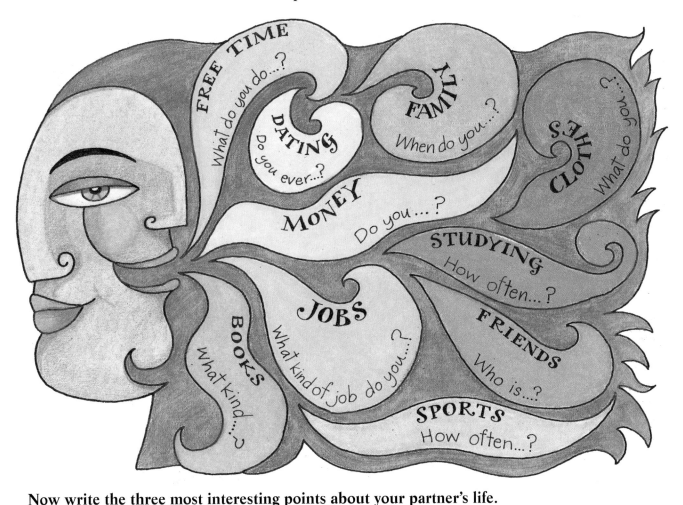

Now write the three most interesting points about your partner's life.

....

....

....

2 **Follow up**
What three things would you like to change about your life?

....

....

....

Compare lists with your partner. Ask your partner
for reasons.

Read And Respond *I'm different now*

▼1 Reading
Read this interview from <u>Lifestyles</u> magazine. Underline two things that have changed.

Interviewer: What was your life like back then?

Andy: Well, five years ago, I was really into traveling —Thailand, Korea, Peru, Zambia, Greece. I just loved moving around and experiencing new things. Usually, I'd spend two or three weeks in one place and then move on. I certainly met a lot of interesting people, but my relationships were very temporary and probably a bit superficial. Thinking about it now, I realize that I never really had any close friends back then. I knew a lot of people, but I didn't know anyone very well.

Interviewer: What's different about you now?

Andy: The main thing is I decided to settle down, to stay in one place. I don't know why I chose Alaska, but it's perfect for me. I'm a carpenter, and I get a lot of satisfaction out of building things. It gives me a sense of accomplishment. Another change is that now I have a handful of very close friends. It feels better to have a couple of deeper relationships instead of a lot of casual ones.

▼2 Try it
Write about your life five years ago. Then on another sheet of paper, write about how your life has changed.

Now

5 years ago

▼3 Shared writing
Work in a group of four. Mix up your paragraphs in two piles. Exchange piles with another group of four. Try to match the "5 years ago" paragraphs and the "Now" paragraphs.

2 PERSONAL HEALTH

- following directions, giving advice
- healthy and unhealthy habits
- imperatives

Warm Up *Health ideas*

What products do people use to stay healthy?
What activities do people do? Work with a
partner. How many can you list?

Ideas
exercise, drinking juice, massage

Products	Activities
....	....
....	....
....	....
....	....
....	....
....	....
....	....

Now look at your list. Circle the most
unusual products and activities. Underline
the most common ones.
Join another pair. Compare lists.

Listening *"Let's relax our minds now"*

Dave Greene has a very stressful job, so he takes a yoga class to relax.

1 **Listening for key words**
Listen. Check the words and phrases as you hear them.

- ☐ relax
- ☐ let go
- ☐ take a deep breath
- ☐ close your eyes
- ☐ open the red door
- ☐ a beautiful garden
- ☐ trees
- ☐ grass
- ☐ river
- ☐ water
- ☐ move your hand

- ☐ an orange door
- ☐ a large kitchen
- ☐ bright and warm
- ☐ fresh bread
- ☐ take a deep breath
- ☐ a bowl of fruit
- ☐ take a big bite
- ☐ bright blue
- ☐ go through the blue door

2 **Listening to imagine**
Listen again with your eyes closed. When the tape stops, write or draw what you imagine.

3 **What do you think?**
Did this exercise help you relax? How?

Conversation Topic *Stress*

1 Vocabulary preview

Which of these activities are stressful for you? Mark them with a +.
Which of these activities reduce stress for you? Mark them with a –.

☐ argue with people
☐ listen to music
☐ see a movie
☐ take a nap
☐ take crowded trains
☐ take my dog for a walk
☐ work too hard
☐ read a book

☐ exercise outdoors
☐ do yoga
☐ take hot baths
☐ take a day off
☐ take long walks
☐ call a friend
☐ play video games

Write one more activity that causes stress for you:

....

Write one more activity that reduces stress for you:

....

2 Conversation building

Read the conversation out loud with a partner.
Change roles and read the conversation again.

Try the conversation again. Use new words from the Vocabulary Preview list.
Now make a new conversation. Use your own ideas.

Grammar Awareness *Take it easy*

Do you have any healthy or unhealthy habits?
What are they?

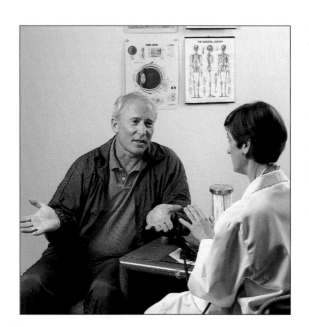

1 Understanding

Dave is talking with his doctor.
Listen. What are Dave's health habits?
Check (✓) True or False.

True	False	
☐	☐	He doesn't smoke cigarettes.
☐	☐	He doesn't drink a lot of alcohol.
☐	☐	He doesn't eat a lot of red meat.
☐	☐	He doesn't worry about things.
☐	☐	He doesn't work too hard.

2 Noticing

The doctor suggests several ways to keep healthy. What are they?
Complete the table. Then listen and check.

Verb	Positive Command	Negative Command
smoke		*Don't smoke any cigarettes*
drink	*Try drinking more fruit juice*	
eat		
take		
worry		
work		

3 Try it

Write two new positive commands and two negative commands about how to stay healthy.

....

....

....

....

....

Grammar Corner
Try to relax more.   *Don't smoke*

18

Pair Interaction *About you*

1 Work with a partner. Your partner will close the book. Ask the questions.
Fill in the chart for your partner.

Do you usually eat healthy food? ....Yes ....No
    What healthy food don't you like? ....
    What unhealthy food do you like? ....

Do you smoke? ....Yes ....No
    (If yes) How much? ....

Do you drink alcohol? ....Yes ....No
    (If yes) How much? ....

Do you worry about things? ....Yes ....No
    How often? ....occasionally ....sometimes ....a lot
    What do you worry about most? ....

Do you work too hard? ....Yes ....No
    Where? (home? job? school?) ....
    When do you have the most stress? ....

Do you get enough sleep? ....Yes ....No
    How much? ....
    When don't you sleep enough? ....

Do you exercise regularly? ....Yes ....No
    How often? ....
    What kind of exercise do you do? ....

> PARDON?
> EXCUSE ME?

When you don't understand, ask.

Now look at all your partner's answers. Rate your partner's health habits.

2 **Follow up**
Now give your partner advice.
Say at least three sentences.
Try to...
Try ___ing... Don't...
I don't think you should...
Now change roles. Your partner will ask about you.

	not so good	OK	good
Food			
Smoking			
Alcohol			
Stress			
Sleep			
Exercise			

Read And Respond *Self-care ideas*

1 ▼ Reading

Read these articles about new health ideas.
Match each article with the best headline.
Which ones might be useful for you?

a. Massage chair
b. Relaxation glasses
c. E-mail health line
d. Acupuncture treatment

☐ Are you the kind of person who has important questions about your health but you're afraid of sounding stupid? Well, now you can ask anything you want without the doctor knowing who you are. Just get on-line and type your questions to Dr. Health. Ask about anything from diet to the most effective ways to relax. Do you want the secrets to good health? Get on your computer and ask Dr. Health. health@csu.md

☐ I'm on my feet all day, and I get back and muscle pain all the time. I'm an absolute wreck by the time I get home. I never thought there would be any hope for me. The first time I tried it, I simply couldn't believe how it made me feel. It completely relaxed me. I sat down, turned it on and for the next 20 minutes I felt like I was in heaven. Now I use it every day as soon as I get home and I'm a new person. It's a great way to unwind after work even if you don't have back pain.

☐ Would you like a relaxing vacation on the beach, but you can't afford the time to travel? The answer is quick and easy: Just put on a pair of these. The world of relaxation that you long for will appear right before your eyes. You see the rich blue-green colors of the ocean, gaze at gentle palm trees swaying in the wind, feel the salty sea breeze against your cheeks...and more. (Not recommended for driving.)

☐ All my life I'd been afraid of needles and never thought they could help me feel better. But the last time I had stomach problems, a friend of mine suggested I see a Chinese specialist who had helped him. I was skeptical at first, but nothing else had worked so I was willing to try anything. Actually, it was painless and much less expensive than my regular doctor.

2 ▼ Try it

Think of an idea for keeping healthy. Explain it in a short paragraph.

....

....

....

3 ▼ Shared writing

Show your paragraph to your partner. Your partner will write a headline for it.
Exchange ideas in a group of four. Which ideas are most popular?

3 LIVING SPACE

- complaining
- neighbor problems
- possessive pronouns

Warm Up *In our city*

**Work with a partner. Think of the three best places in your area to live.
Rank them and explain why.**

	Place	Reason
1.		
2.		
3.		

**Now compare answers with another pair.
Do you agree? Why or why not?**

Listening *"It's really a problem"*

Nick and Mrs. Chen are neighbors. Mrs. Chen has a problem.

1 ▸ Listening for key words
Listen. Check the words and phrases you hear.

☐ worried about the noise
☐ worried about your friends

☐ it's probably my cousins
☐ it's probably my friends

☐ from our apartment
☐ from the neighbors

☐ talk very loud
☐ shut the door

☐ every night
☐ late at night

☐ ask them to leave
☐ ask them to be more quiet

2 ▸ Listening for meaning
Listen again. What is Mrs. Chen complaining about?

....

What is Nick going to do?

....

3 ▸ What do you think?
Is Mrs. Chen angry with Nick? Why do you think so?

Conversation Topic *Neighbors*

1 Vocabulary preview

Which of these neighbor problems are serious?
Rank them 1-10. 1 = not serious, 10 = very serious

.... their dog barks late at night

.... they park their car in your parking space

.... they leave garbage outside

.... they don't say hello to you

.... they watch what you are doing

.... they make a lot of noise

.... they don't take care of their yard

.... they don't return things they borrow

.... their pets make a mess

.... they argue a lot

your own idea: ....

2 Conversation building

Read the conversation out loud with a partner.
Change roles and read the conversation again.

Try the conversation again. Use new words from the Vocabulary Preview list.
Now make a new conversation. Use your own ideas.

Grammar Awareness *A messy apartment*

Here is Laura's apartment. Is your place similar or different? In what way?

1 Understanding

**Laura is talking about things in the apartment.
Listen. Who owns each thing?
Make a check in the correct column.**

Items	Laura	Melissa	Tom
a bicycle in the hall	....	....	....
hiking boots under the table	....	....	....
clothes on the couch	....	....	....
magazines on the table	....	....	....
paints on the floor	....	....	....
clothes next to the door	....		....

2 Noticing

Fill in the missing words. Then listen again and check.

Julie: Is the bicycle in the hall Melissa's?

Laura: No, that's not .... It belongs to her boyfriend, Tom. He comes here a lot.

Julie: And these hiking boots under the table? Are they his too?

Laura: Yeah, they're ....

Julie: How about these clothes on the couch? Are they Melissa's or yours?

Laura: Those are ....

Julie: How about all these magazines on the table?

Laura: Oh, some of them are .... , but most of them are ....

Julie: And the paints on the floor? I guess they're ....

Laura: No, I keep .... in my own room. Those are ....

Julie: Whose?

Laura: Tom's...he's a painter...or, at least, he thinks he is.

Julie: How about those clothes next to the door?

Laura: Oh, those are ....

Julie: You mean, ... and Melissa's?

3 Try it

Work with a partner. Put two personal items on one desk. Write four sentences.

The pencil is mine.

....

....

....

Grammar Corner			
my room	mine	*her* things	hers
your place	yours	*our* apartment	ours
his things	his	*their* clothes	theirs

Pair Interaction *Planning a neighborhood*

You and your partner are going to design a neighborhood.
Look at the grid below. What do you want in your neighborhood?

1 **Tear or cut out the squares on page 97.** These are the neighborhood pieces.
Decide which items you want. Decide where to put each item.

• You must put something on each space.
• Each item costs "points." The points are written on the item. You can spend only 25 points.
• You must have: **shops** - at least 2 squares, no more than 4 squares
              green space - at least 3 squares
              public service - at least 2 squares
              restaurants and entertainment - at least 3 squares, not more than 5 squares

Your apartment

2 **Follow up**
Describe your neighborhood to another pair.
Explain your choices.

I WANT A
____ BECAUSE...

Add more information.

Example
We decided to put the video store next to
our house because we like to rent movies.

Read And Respond *There's no place like home*

1 Reading

Read this article from <u>Practical Living</u> magazine. Find three ways to improve a small living space.

Want To Change Your Living Environment?

Here are three inexpensive suggestions

When I first moved into my apartment, I felt it was way too small and unlivable. But I found there are some things I can do to make it not only comfortable, but also personal.

One thing I do regularly is change the posters and pictures on my walls. I try to never keep anything in the same place for more than a year. Sometimes, I move them to a different wall or I put them away for a while and get new ones. This is an inexpensive way to add color and life to my apartment, without taking up too much space.

Another thing I do is throw things away! Old magazines and books, clothes I don't wear, things I've collected - anything I'm not using, I get rid of. Every six months I go through everything I own and ruthlessly divide what is important from what I can do without.

One of my favorite things to do is buy flowers. Every Friday afternoon, I buy fresh flowers and put them in a small vase on my table. Not only does this change the look of my place, it puts me in a good mood for the weekend!

These things are simple, but they help me feel comfortable and at home.

2 Try it

Write an article for <u>Practical Living</u> magazine. Explain some simple, inexpensive ways to change the appearance of your apartment or room.

....

....

....

3 Shared writing

Work in a group of four. Read each other's ideas. Which are the most practical? Which would you use in your own home?

Group Activity *The match game*

How much do you and your classmates have in common? First answer these questions.

What is…

1 a free time activity you like?

2 a place or building in your neighborhood?

3 something that makes you feel stressed?

4 a type or style of clothing you like?

5 a place you often go?

6 one word that describes your room?

7 a problem with the place you live?

8 a good health habit you have?

9 a bad health habit you have?

10 one word that describes your lifestyle?

11 a good way for you to deal with stress?

12 something that other people do that you don't like?

Now work in a group of three. Compare answers.

If all three people gave the same answer, you each get two points.
If two people gave the same answer, you each get one point.
If you all have different answers, you get no points.

Your points: ....

Learning Check

1 Grammar Check 🔲

Julie is talking to her brother, Jordan. Fill in the missing words.
You may use some words more than once.
Then listen to the conversation to check your answers.

are	borrow	do	don't	mine
stop	too	use	wear	yours

Julie: Jordan, you're driving me crazy! [_____] taking my things. [_____] your own.

Jordan: What do you mean?

Julie: Like this notebook computer. It's [_____]. It's not [_____].

Jordan: Oh, sorry. [_____] is at school, so I had to use [_____].

Julie: And [_____] [_____] my clothes.

Jordan: You mean that blue sweatshirt of [_____]?

Julie: Yeah. [_____] your own.

Jordan; Sorry, I was going to a party and I couldn't find [_____].

Julie. Well, just [_____] [_____] it again. I just don't understand it. Laura's always using my things and now you [_____] [_____]. You two should get together some time.

2 Vocabulary Expansion - Idioms

Read the sentences. Fill in the blanks.

out of hand	check out	crazy	get along
hanging around	into	stay in shape	

1. Nick and Jordan are both _____ about movies. They go to the movies every weekend.

2. Julie is really _____ her new job. She stays at the office late every night.

3. Nick and Jordan like _____ in music stores.

   They like to _____ the newest CDs. They both have a lot of CDs.

4. Nick and his parents don't _____ very well. They don't talk to each other often.

5. Jordan exercises a lot because he wants to _____. He likes being healthy.

6. Nick's cousins get a little _____ at night. They make a lot of noise.

Now say the meaning of each idiom in different words.

Review Game *Conversation spiral*

Work in groups of three or four. Take turns. Move around the board. When you land on a square, answer the question. The first person to answer 10 questions wins.

Each person needs a space marker. Put it on the START space. Close your eyes. Touch the HOW MANY SPACES box with a pencil. Move that many spaces. Answer the question. Each player can answer each question only one time.

How Many Spaces

1	2	3
2	3	1
3	2	1

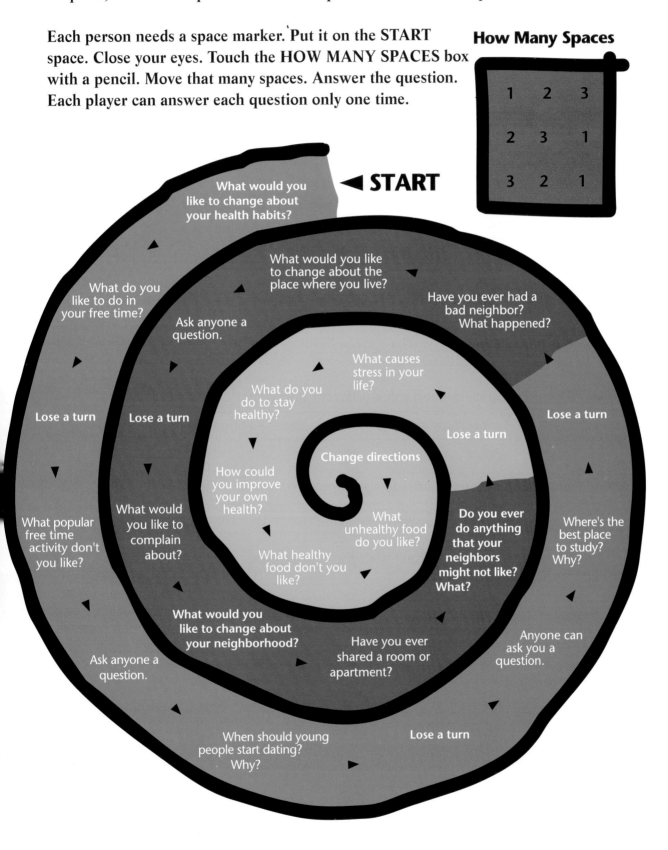

◄ START

What would you like to change about your health habits?

What would you like to change about the place where you live?

Have you ever had a bad neighbor? What happened?

What do you like to do in your free time?

Ask anyone a question.

What causes stress in your life?

What do you do to stay healthy?

Lose a turn

Lose a turn

Lose a turn

Lose a turn

Change directions

How could you improve your own health?

What unhealthy food do you like?

Do you ever do anything that your neighbors might not like? What?

Where's the best place to study? Why?

What popular free time activity don't you like?

What would you like to complain about?

What healthy food don't you like?

What would you like to change about your neighborhood?

Have you ever shared a room or apartment?

Anyone can ask you a question.

Ask anyone a question.

When should young people start dating? Why?

Lose a turn

Learning Better *Develop your conversations*

1 **Do you think this is a "good" conversation? Why or why not?**

One way to develop a conversation is to <u>add extra information.</u>

> Do you like movies?   Yes. I go to movies two or three times a week!

Answer these questions. Add extra information:

> Do you like movies?

> Your answer .... Extra information

> What are your favorite movies?

> Your answer .... Extra information

> How often do you go to the movies?

> Your answer .... Extra information

Try it again.

This time, answer the question and <u>ask a different question.</u>

> Do you like movies?   Yes, how about you? What movies do you like?

Once more.

This time, answer the question and <u>add your opinion.</u>

> Do you like movies?   Yes, but I think a lot of movies are too violent.

ADD MORE   ASK ANOTH QUESTION   ADD YOU OPINION

Now try it. Work with a partner. Start with these questions:

> Do you like sports?

> Do you like learning English?

Keep going. Whenever you answer a question...

2 **Learning better task**

This week, notice a conversation in your first language. What do you do to develop your conversation — to "keep the conversation going"? Write some ideas.

What you do in your first language to "keep going"

Which of these "strategies" can you also try in English conversation?

4 FAMILY HISTORY

- telling a story
- life achievements
- used to, simple present tense

Warm Up *Family relationships*

Work with a partner. Write down all of the family relationship words you know.

mother ....

father ....

....

....

....

....

....

....

Now join another pair.
How many of your words are the same?

Listening *"They left all that behind"*

Nick is talking about his family background.

▼1 Listening for key words
Listen. Check the words and phrases you hear.

- ☐ a Japanese name
- ☐ from Brazil
- ☐ my father's parents moved
- ☐ my mother's parents moved
- ☐ northern Japan
- ☐ start a new life
- ☐ take a chance

- ☐ took everything with them
- ☐ left everything behind
- ☐ house
- ☐ friends and relatives
- ☐ start a farm
- ☐ started a fruit and vegetable business
- ☐ a lot of problems at first
- ☐ no problems at first

▼2 Listening for meaning
Listen again. What is the Koda family story? Circle the answers.

Nick's grandparents were from
  a. northern Japan
  b. central Japan

They used to be
  a. rice farmers
  b. business people

When they were in their 20s, they moved to
  a. the United States
  b. Brazil

When they first moved, they
  a. had a lot of problems
  b. made a lot of friends

They started
  a. an import business
  b. a fruit and vegetable business

▼3 What do you think?
Is Nick happy with the decision his grandparents made? Why do you think so?

Conversation Topic *Family background*

1 Vocabulary preview

Think about your family. Write a name and a place next to each life event.

someone who:	who	where
graduated from high school		
had a difficult job		
got married many years ago		
was born in an unusual place		
moved to another place		
graduated from college		
your own idea:		

2 Conversation building

Read the conversation out loud with a partner.
Change roles and read the conversation again.

Now make a new conversation. Use real information about your own family.

Grammar Awareness *For better or for worse*

The Chen family came to the United States from China in 1988. How do you think they like living in the States?

▼1 Understanding
Listen to Mrs. Chen. How has the Chens' life changed? Complete the table.

China	United States
1. lived in a two-room apartment	....
2. went to work by bicycle	....
3.	spend their free time watching TV
4.	work eight hours a day
5. do the washing by hand	....
6.	feel afraid

Do you think the Chens' life has changed for the better or the worse?

▼2 Noticing
Fill in the verbs in these sentences. Then listen again and check.

1. We .... in a two-room apartment, but now we .... in a six-room apartment.
2. I .... to work by bicycle, but now I .... my car to work.
3. We .... our free time in China reading and talking, but now we .... our free time watching TV.
4. I .... 12 hours a day. Here I .... eight hours a day.
5. Our family .... the house and do the washing by hand. Now we .... a lot of machines to help us.
6. In China we .... completely safe. But now we .... frightened of the crime and violence here.

▼3 Try it
Write three sentences about what you used to do and what you do now.

I used to .... but now I ....

I used to .... but now I ....

I used to .... but now I ....

Grammar Corner
I used to play soccer but now I just watch it.

Pair Interaction *Family history tic-tac-toe*

For Additional Games
go to page 99

1 Work with a partner. Use one book. Pick a square.
Ask your partner a question about the information in that square.
When your partner answers, write his or her name on the square. If your partner can't
answer, you get the square. If you get three in a row, you win that game!
(For additional games, go to page 99.)

Your Family

YOUR MOTHER	YOUR BROTHER	YOUR SISTER
YOUR PET	YOU	ASK ANY QUESTION
THE BUSIEST PERSON IN YOUR FAMILY	YOUR FATHER	THE NICEST PERSON IN YOUR FAMILY

2 **Follow up**
Think of a famous family in your country.
How many facts can you say about them?
Try to list five.

When you don't understand, ask.

ONCE MORE PLEASE? COULD YOU REPEAT THAT?

Read And Respond *A star is born*

1 Reading
Read about William Shakespeare's family. Complete the family tree.

When John Shakespeare married Mary Arden in 1562, they didn't know that their third child would become the most famous writer in the English language. John was a prosperous businessman, who owned a glove-making factory near Stratford. Mary was the daughter of a wealthy landowner in the neighboring village of Wilmacote.

In April 1564, their eldest son, William, was born in Stratford-upon-Avon. Not much is known about William's early life. In December 1582, he married Ann Hathaway, the daughter of a farmer. Their first child, Susanna, was born in May 1583. In February 1585, Ann gave birth to twins — Hamnet and Judith.

Shakespeare's early interest in theater led him to London, where he spent much of his life away from his family in Stratford. In London, William became the best known playwright of his time. In his life, he wrote 37 plays, the best known of which are <u>Romeo and Juliet</u> and <u>Hamlet</u>. He also wrote a large number of poems. He only returned to Stratford to live with the family for the last four years of his life.

When Shakespeare died in 1616, he was survived by his wife and his two daughters. His son, Hamnet, had died in 1596.

```
┌─────────────┐       ┌─────────────┐
│             │  and  │             │
└──────┬──────┘       └─────────────┘
       │
  William Shakespeare   and   ┌─────────────┐
       born: ........               │             │
       died: ........               └──────┬──────┘
       ┌────────────────────┼────────────────────┐
  ┌─────────────┐    ┌─────────────┐    ┌─────────────┐
  │             │    │             │    │             │
  └─────────────┘    └─────────────┘    └─────────────┘
  born: ........     born: ........      born: ........
                     died: 1596
```

2 Try it
Choose a famous person (living or dead). Write a brief family history but leave out the person's name.

....

....

....

3 Shared writing
Make a group of four. Read each other's family histories. Can you guess who the person is?

IMPORTANT PEOPLE

- talking about change, evaluating
- verb tenses
- personal events

Warm Up *Famous people*

Work in a group of three.
How many famous people can you name?
You have one minute for each category.

Music

Art

Literature

Religion

Science

Politics

Compare your answers with another group.
How many of your names are the same?

Listening *"He had a big influence on my life"*

Jordan and his father, Dave, are looking at some of Dave's old photos.

1 Listening for key words
Listen. Check the words and phrases you hear.

- ☐ your girlfriend
- ☐ your friend

- ☐ find someone who
- ☐ try something new

- ☐ take life more seriously
- ☐ take music more seriously

- ☐ found someone new
- ☐ found somebody else

- ☐ moved to London
- ☐ moved from London

- ☐ found me my first real job
- ☐ gave me my first real break

- ☐ dumped you
- ☐ jumped you

- ☐ had a big part
- ☐ had a big influence

- ☐ started in journalism
- ☐ started working for him

2 Listening for meaning
Listen again. Why were these people important in Dave's life?

Person	Influence on David
• Mary	*After she... he ....*
• Eric	*He taught Dave...*
• Phil	*He gave Dave...*

3 What do you think?
Which of these people do you think was most important in Dave's life? Why do you think so

Conversation Topic *Influences*

1 Vocabulary preview

Look at the list of people. Choose four who were important in your life. Write their names.
What was their influence on you? Look at the list for ideas.

Name	People	Influence
....	a teacher	told me I was smart
....	a friend	showed me some new places
....	my first boyfriend/ girlfriend	made me feel happy
....	a relative	gave me good advice
....	a boss	gave me confidence
....	a co-worker	gave me a good job
....	a hero	encouraged me to read serious books
....	a famous person	encouraged me to try harder
		your own idea: ....

2 Conversation building

Read the conversation out loud with a partner.
Change roles and read the conversation again.

Try the conversation again. Use new words from the Vocabulary Preview list.
Now make a new conversation. Use your own ideas.

Grammar Awareness *My favorite musician*

Who is your favorite musician?

1 Understanding
**Listen to Dave Greene talk about one of his favorite artists, Eric Clapton.
Then answer the questions.**

1. What kind of life has Eric Clapton had?
2. When did his son die?
3. What is he enjoying now?
4. What does he do every year in London?

2 Noticing
**Write the verbs in the correct tense.
Then listen to check.**

Eric Clapton is one of Britain's most successful rock and blues guitarists ever. In 1993 he (win) .... six Grammy awards. He (play) .... in several legendary rock bands, including *Cream,* and (develop) .... a versatile playing style. Every year he (give) .... a series of concerts in London's famous Albert Hall.

Clapton's life (be) .... easy. He (be) .... a drug addict and an alcoholic for many years, but he (recover) .... He married and (divorce) .... twice. In 1991 he (lose) .... his four-year-old son, Conor, when he fell out of a 53rd-floor window in Manhattan. Despite his difficulties, Clapton (create) .... some of the best rock-blues of all time.

Clapton admits that he (find) .... it hard to be in the public spotlight but says he is basically happy. Meanwhile he (enjoy) .... his music more than ever and (carry) .... on singing the blues.

3 Try it
Write three sentences about the life of someone you admire.

....

....

....

....

....

Grammar Corner
Past Simple - *My son died in 1991.*
Present Perfect - *I have been drug free since 1985.*
Present Continuous - *I am enjoying myself more now.*
Present Simple - *I give a series of concerts at the Albert Hall every year.*
Future - *I am going to carry on singing the blues.*

For Guest Cards
go to page 101

Pair Interaction *VIP party*

1 You and your partner are planning a party. The guests will be VIPs (Very Important People). Who will you invite? What questions will you ask each VIP?

Step 1.

- Tear out the VIP guest cards on page 101. 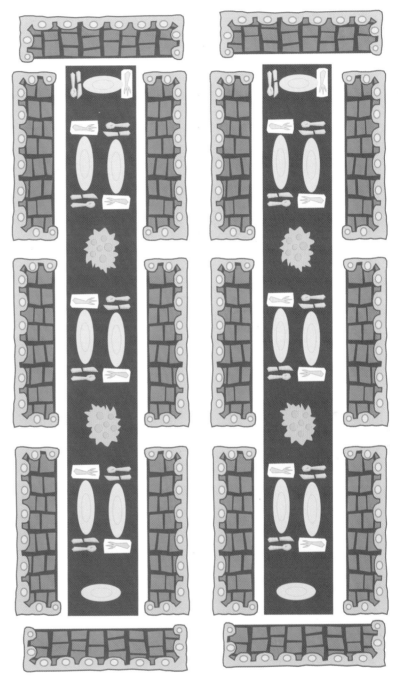 Put all the cards on the table in front of you.
- Together, choose 15 people to invite (15 cards). Write each guest's name on a card.
- Think of two questions you want to ask each guest. Write the questions on the card.

Step 2.

There will be a dinner party. Decide where everyone will sit at a large table. Remember, some guests may not want to talk to other guests. Lay out your cards so that everyone is sitting near someone they want to talk to. Don't forget to decide where you and your partner will sit.

WHAT..? WHERE..?
WHY..? WHO..?

Ask WH - questions.

2 **Follow up**

There has been a change of plans. Now you can invite only 10 people. Decide which 10 guests to invite.

Read And Respond *Who's who?*

1 Reading

Read these descriptions of four famous people.
Underline the parts that describe their main influence on other people.

Charlotte Bronte
(1816-1855)

The daughter of an English church family, she wrote seven novels and inspired generations of women to take up the craft of writing. Jane Eyre was her most widely read book. Her heroes and heroines were inspired not only by her vivid imagination but also by her powers of perception. She was a meticulous observer of people and their ways, which gave her work an overpowering sense of accuracy and realism.

Charles Darwin
(1809-1882)

Very few scientists have inspired the kind of heated controversies that this man's work provoked. His observations on the lonely Galapagos Islands off the coast of Ecuador made him famous, but they also created controversies about humanity's beginnings — issues that still anger people and incite politicians and religious leaders across the world.

Billie Holiday
(1915-1959)

Her life was full of suffering and pain, but she translated her heartache into songs that moved millions. Inspiring generations of singers who came after her, she is probably more popular now than when she was alive. It's hard to imagine a woman's voice that is more recognizable and well-known.

Pablo Picasso
(1881-1973)

Like a magnificent earthquake, the invention of the camera shook the foundations of the art world, and this artist was among the first to pick up the pieces. What he did with those pieces, rearranging and recombining them, changed forever the way we would appreciate and evaluate painting. Few artists in history have had this kind of impact or influence.

2 Try it

Think of a famous person you admire.
Write an encyclopedia entry but don't write the person's name.

3 Shared writing

Show your entry to members of your group. Can you guess the person?
Which one was the most interesting?

6 PERSONALITY

- expressing opinions, describing people
- characteristics
- relative clauses

Warm Up *My personality*

Check (✓) the items that are true for you.
Then work with a partner.
Ask your partner the questions.
Circle your partner's answers.

Would you rather…

watch comedy TV shows	**or**	watch serious TV shows
get up early on weekends		sleep late on weekends
go to a small party (fewer than 10 people)		go to a large party (more than 20 people)
try hang-gliding		watch hang-gliding
talk to new people at a party		listen to other people
be busy		have nothing to do

Now check two words that best describe your partner.

energetic	easy-going
serious	talkative
free-spirited	careful
outgoing	reserved
studious	wild

Now add one more. ....

**What words did your partner say about you?
Do you agree?**

Listening *"I thought you were..."*

Jordan and Laura are on a date. They're talking about their first impressions.

1 Listening for key words
Listen. Check the words and phrases you hear.

- [ ] it was fun
- [ ] talked to a guy
- [ ] talk too much
- [ ] quiet
- [ ] boring
- [ ] bored
- [ ] an airhead
- [ ] didn't say anything

- [ ] cautious
- [ ] a jerk
- [ ] about yourself
- [ ] about lots of things
- [ ] self-centered
- [ ] aggressive
- [ ] gentle
- [ ] nervous

2 Listening for meaning
Listen again. Complete the table.

what Laura thought about Jordan before	what Laura knows about Jordan now
what Jordan thought about Laura before	what Jordan knows about Laura now

3 What do you think?
What does Jordan like about Laura?
What does Laura like about Jordan?

✿ Conversation Topic *Characteristics* 📼

Vocabulary preview
Look at the actions. Match each one with a characteristic.

Actions	Characteristics
tells funny stories	entertaining
spends a lot of time at the library	sociable
cleans up all the time	reserved
has a lot of parties at her house	thoughtful
talks a lot	studious
sends birthday cards to all her friends	neat
tries new things	chatty
keeps things to herself (himself)	adventurous
talks about new ideas	interesting
your own idea:	

Conversation building
Read the conversation out loud with a partner.
Change roles and read the conversation again.

Try the conversation again. Use new words from the Vocabulary Preview list.
Now make a new conversation. Use your own ideas.

Grammar Awareness *Advice for Jordan*

Do you sometimes feel anxious in your language class? What makes you feel anxious?

▶1 Understanding

Read these sentences. Then listen to Jordan talking to his language teacher. Which are true about Jordan? Check yes or no.

I feel confident when speaking in class.
☐ yes ☐ no
I worry about making mistakes in class.
☐ yes ☐ no
I always think other students are better than me.
☐ yes ☐ no
I always try to answer questions in class.
☐ yes ☐ no
I think other students will laugh at me.
☐ yes ☐ no

Is Jordan an anxious language learner?

▶2 Noticing

Complete these sentences. Then listen again to check.

An anxious learner is { someone / a person / a student } {
who .... when speaking.
who .... mistakes.
who .... are better.
who .... questions in class.
who .... laugh at him or her.
}

▶3 Try it

Now write some definitions of a confident learner. Here is one to start you off.

A confident learner is someone who is not afraid of speaking.

....

....

....

Grammar Corner
An anxious language learner is a person <u>who worries about mistakes in class</u>

Pair Interaction *Personality types*

1 Work with a partner. Look at these people. What do you imagine they are like?
Write one personality word for each person.

free-spirited	entertaining	adventurous	fiery
conservative	honest	ambitious	intriguing
bright	playful	competitive	serious
confident	stimulating	creative	wild
delicate	funny	earthy	unusual

**Use your imagination.
Give your opinions and ideas.**

**Now choose one person. Imagine more details
about that person.**

name: ....

where he or she lives: ....

more about his or her personality (give examples): ....

....

things he or she likes: ....

a problem he or she has: ....

2 **Follow up**
Join another pair. Tell about your character.

Read And Respond *When we first met*

▼1 Reading

Read Laura's journal entry about her first impression of Jordan.
What did Laura think about him at first? What does she think now?

May 15th

*Today a friend asked me about when Jordan and I first met.
I had to laugh because it made me remember the first
impression I had of him. To be honest, I didn't really like
him at first. He seemed very egotistical then. I felt
uncomfortable being around him. He talked the whole time
and when I didn't say anything, he just sat there like he was
evaluating me. I hated that. I also remember the ugly shoes
he had on.*

*I don't know exactly when I started to like him. I think I
just got to know him better and learned that he was actually
a sweetheart. I think he was just nervous the first time we
met. The next time he listened more and showed more interest
in me. Now I feel really good talking to him. He's actually
very open and gentle, but I certainly didn't get that
impression in the beginning.*

▼2 Try it

What was your first impression of one of your close friends? Write about the things
you noticed or felt.

▼3 Shared writing

Exchange papers with a partner. Describe how your relationship with your friend
developed.

Group Activity *Find someone who...*

Stand up. Work with a partner. Ask a question.
If your partner says no, ask a different question.
If your partner says yes, write your partner's name.
When you answer yes, add extra information. Then find a new partner.

Use each name only one time.

Find someone who...	Name	Extra information
... has a friend in another country. *(Do you have a friend in another country?)*		
... has been on TV. *(Have you been...?)*		
... has a relative over 90 years old. *(Do you ...?)*		
... has a friend who is "wild."		
... has a neighbor who is a "jerk."		
... has a pet for a best friend.		
... does yoga to relax.		
... is studious.		
... has heard an Eric Clapton song.		
... is an anxious language learner.		
... has an unusual job.		
... has read a play by William Shakespearc.		
... would like to become famous.		

Learning Check

1 Grammar Check

Read the sentences. Six are correct. Six have mistakes.
If a sentence is correct, check (✓) OK. If a sentence has a mistake, correct it.
(bet)

1. The Chens used to living in a two-bedroom apartment but now they live in a big house. ☐ OK?
2. Every year Eric Clapton gives a series of concerts in London. ☐ OK?
3. An anxious person is someone who thinks people are always laughing at her. ☐ OK?
4. Mrs. Chen used travel to work by bicycle, but now she drives a car. ☐ OK?
5. Eric Clapton is recorded some of the best rock-blues of all time. ☐ OK?
6. An anxious person is someone who she worries a lot. ☐ OK?
7. Mrs. Chen used to work 12 hours a day but now she works only eight hours a day. ☐ OK?
8. Eric Clapton has won six Grammy awards in 1993. ☐ OK?
9. A confident person is someone who has a good image of herself. ☐ OK?
10. Mrs. Chen used to wash clothes by hand but now she uses a washing machine. ☐ OK?
11. Eric Clapton lost his son in 1991. ☐ OK?
12. A confident person is someone likes meeting new people. ☐ OK?

Grammar Market

How sure are you? You have $1000 to bet. You must bet on six sentences.
How much will you bet on each sentence ($100 to $500)?
Now work in a group of four. Compare your answers. Decide which are correct.

• If you were wrong you lose your "bet money" for that sentence.
• If you were correct, you win your "bet money" for that sentence.

Now check your answers with your teacher to be sure.
Who in your group "won" the most money?

2 Vocabulary expansion

Look at these faces. Which person is the happiest? Write #1 next to the person. Which person is the least happy? Write #5. Then number the other people 2, 3, 4.

☐ Jordan ☐ Nick ☐ Julie ☐ Lynn ☐ Laura

Now complete the sentences with the correct words: completely, really, pretty, sort of, a little

Jordan is .... happy.   Nick is .... happy.   Julie is .... happy.
Lynn is .... happy.   Laura is .... happy.

Now write some sentences about yourself. Choose some characteristics below.
Add completely, really, pretty, sort of, or a little.

shy	easy-going	free-spirited	studious	wild
chatty	interesting	sociable	entertaining	reserved

Review Game *Talking marathon*

Step 1:
Think of someone you admire or respect.

How long can you talk about the person?
You have one minute to think about what
to say.
- who is this person?
- what has the person done?
- what is this person like?
- why do you respect this person?

Step 2:
Now work with a partner.
Talk about the person.
How long can you speak without stopping?

    Start like this:
    I really respect _____ .

Partner, listen. Check the time.
The turn is over when:
- The speaker pauses (stops) for five seconds.
- The speaker says a word that is not English.
  *(Of course, names of people and places
  might not be in English.)*

Step 3:
When the turn is over, the listener asks
two questions.

Step 4:
Change roles. The first listener becomes
the speaker and talks about his or her topic.

Step 5:
When you finish, find a new partner.
Talk about your topic again. Add more
information.

51

Learning Better *Think about how you learn vocabulary*

1 **Work with a partner. Look at the pictures.**
Match each description with the correct picture.

1. He puts English labels on things in his house.

2. She's testing herself with vocabulary cards.

3. She's relaxing and listening to music while studying new vocabulary.

4. He draws a picture next to each vocabulary word.

5. He's making sentences and stories with the new vocabulary words.

6. She's trying to use new words in conversation.

Here are some words and phrases from Units 4-6. Which strategy above could you use to learn
each one? Write the number next to the words and phrases.

☐ take a chance   ☐ a real break

☐ start a business   ☐ dumped me

☐ a big influence   ☐ an airhead

☐ encourage   ☐ chatty

☐ self-centered   ☐ leave everything behind

☐ keeps things to herself/himself   ☐ feel anxious

2 **Learning better task**
Choose five words you want to learn. Write them in the table.
Think of a strategy to learn each word.

Words	Strategy

This week try some of the strategies above to learn your five words.

- reasons, comparisons
- consumer items
- past modal "should have"

Warm Up *Shopping list*

Work with a partner. Think of the things you buy regularly. Write at least three items for each category.

Personal Care
- *shampoo*
-
-
-

Food
- *potato chips*
-
-
-

Clothing
- *T-shirts*
-
-
-

Entertainment
- *magazines*
-
-
-

Household
- *dish soap*
-
-
-

Gifts
- *greeting card*
-
-
-

School
- *notebook*
-
-
-

Other
- *train pass*
-
-
-

Now join two other pairs. Read your lists. Circle all the items that more than one person says.

Listening *TV commercials*

Nick is watching TV at home.

1 Listening for key words

Listen to the TV commercials. Check the words and phrases you hear.

1.
- [ ] I'm beautiful
- [ ] you can't be beautiful
- [ ] you can be beautiful
- [ ] shampoo
- [ ] soap
- [ ] soft, attractive

2.
- [ ] our first kiss
- [ ] the kisser's toothpaste
- [ ] tastes great
- [ ] kisses great
- [ ] smell fresh
- [ ] gentle
- [ ] Teen Girl magazine

3.
- [ ] strong man
- [ ] scent
- [ ] sweat
- [ ] sweet
- [ ] strength

2 Listening for meaning

Listen again. What does each product do?
Check the correct answer.

1. Night Beauty
- [ ] makes your hair soft
- [ ] makes your hair dark
- [ ] makes you jealous

2. Tooth Love
- [ ] helps you get a date
- [ ] makes your breath fresh
- [ ] makes you a good kisser

3. Strong Man
- [ ] makes you strong
- [ ] makes you sweat
- [ ] makes you smell strong

3 What do you think?

Which of these advertisements is the funniest?
What makes it funny?

Conversation Topic *Things to buy*

1 Vocabulary preview

Match each item below with a reason for buying it.

Items	Reasons
a hair dryer	getting really tense
a pocket tape recorder	traveling a lot
a pair of contact lenses	in a hurry in the morning
an alarm clock	missing meetings
a massage chair	thinking about my appearance
a bottle of vitamins	oversleeping
a pager	feeling out of energy
an airline carry-on bag	thinking of new ideas
an electronic dictionary	missing messages
an appointment book	coming across new words
your own idea:	

2 Conversation building

Read the conversation out loud with a partner.
Change roles and read the conversation again.

Try the conversation again. Use new words from the Vocabulary Preview list.
Now make a new conversation. Use your own ideas.

55

Grammar Awareness *Jordan's shopping trip*

What are the three most useful pieces of furniture in your home?

1 Understanding

Jordan went shopping for furniture for his apartment. Listen and check the things he bought.

☐ kitchen table   ☐ bed
☐ coffee table   ☐ chest of drawers
☐ desk   ☐ kitchen chairs
☐ armchair   ☐ floor lamp
☐ sofa   ☐ potted plant

2 Noticing

What are the pieces of furniture that Jordan should have bought? Complete these sentences. Then listen to check.

1. He should _____ .
2. He should _____ .
3. He _____ .
4. He _____ .
5. He _____ .

3 Try it

Think of a time you went shopping — for clothes, food, or things for your apartment. What did you buy? What should you have bought? Write three sentences.

I bought some ice cream, but I should have bought yogurt.

_____

_____

_____

Grammar Corner
She should have bought a table.
She should have bought a lamp.

Pair Interaction *Speaking of shopping*

1 Work with a partner. Choose any square. Read it.
Your partner will answer the question. Then cross it out (✗).

What is your favorite store? Why?

What's a good place to go window shopping? (JUST LOOKING, NOT BUYING.)

Have you ever sold anything? What? Where? SOLD

What is something you really want to buy? 1042 775

OUR STORE Tell about an unusual store.

BOO·TIQUE What store don't you like?

SALE What's something good that happened to you while shopping?

What's the most expensive thing you've bought?

Tell about a time you got a good deal. (BOUGHT SOMETHING FOR A VERY GOOD PRICE!) 10¢

Tell about an unusual advertisement or TV commercial. Did you like it or not?

What's something bad that happened to you while shopping?

Tell about something you bought that you later regretted. (IT WAS A MISTAKE!)

2 **Follow up**
With your partner, decide the best store in your city
for each of these things. Why do you think so?

clothing   gifts

        books   stationery

electrical appliances   food

WHAT...?
WHERE...?
WHEN...?
WHY...?

**Get more information.
Ask WH-Questions.**

57

Read And Respond *Miracle product*

 ## Reading

Read this advertisement for Juba. Where can you find an advertisement like this? What is "Juba"? Would you buy it? Why or why not?

HOW IS YOUR MEMORY? COULD IT BE BETTER? TRY JUBA!

Is it ever hard for you to remember phone numbers, jokes, people's birthdays? Do you often have trouble with new information because you just can't remember what you heard or read?

There is help for you. It's called Juba — which means "magic." Juba is a small rectangular patch that you put on the soft skin just behind your ear. After just 20 minutes a patented, all-natural ingredient is absorbed through your skin. It then reacts with your natural body chemistry to increase your memory a remarkable 100%! Other advantageous effects are increased energy and an increase in overall alertness.

Juba was developed after more than 20 years of high-level research at our private laboratories and is now available to consumers around the world. What is astounding is that it is derived naturally and by means of a process that is completely safe and non-polluting.

Listen to this personal testimony:

"This product is sensational. I tried it while I was studying Spanish and I memorized complete vocabulary lists and hundreds of complicated grammar rules."
- Mary Makoni

THE JUBA PATCH IS SAFE AND RELIABLE! ORDER IT TODAY!

Available from Juba Laboratories, P. O. Box 235, Los Angeles, California 96000 USA

 ## Try it

Think of a "miracle" product. Think of an interesting name for it. Write an advertisement for the product.

 ## Shared writing

Make a group of four. Read each other's advertisements. Choose the best advertisement and suggest how to make it even better.

8 MYSTERIES

- describing past events
- unusual events
- past simple and past continuous

Warm Up *What happened?*

**Work with a partner. Read each situation.
Can you explain the mystery?
Write your reasons.**

Someone sent me a present, but there
was no card.
Maybe...

The phone rang, but no one was there.
Maybe ...

The train didn't stop at my station.
Perhaps...

A person I didn't know kept smiling at me.
Perhaps...

The TV turned off even though I didn't
touch it.
Probably...

I was thinking about someone, and just
then they phoned me.
Maybe...

**Join two more pairs. Compare reasons.
Have any of these happened to you?**

Listening *"I never thought I'd find it"*

Julie is talking to her mother, Lynn.

1 Listening for key statements
Listen. Check the sentences that are true.

☐ Julie found an old earring.
☐ Julie found an old necklace.

☐ She found it under a chair.
☐ She found it in the garden.

☐ Lynn lost it 30 years ago.
☐ Lynn's mother lost it 60 years ago.

☐ Lynn's mother was angry at Lynn.
☐ Lynn was angry at her mother.

2 Listening for meaning
How did the earring get lost? Write your answer.

....

....

....

3 What do you think?
How does Lynn feel about what Julie found?

Conversation Topic *Unusual events*

1 Vocabulary preview

Look at these ordinary events. Match them with a reason that makes them unusual.

Events	Why is it unusual
I ran into an old friend.	I only studied for one month.
I found an old watch.	I have no idea who it's from.
I received some flowers.	I thought he (she) was dead.
The lights went out at home.	I don't know who sent them.
I had a dream about you.	My mother lost it 40 years ago.
I got a present in the mail.	There was no storm.
I passed the English proficiency test.	It had a rare postage stamp on it.
I bought an old necklace at a garage sale.	It turned out to have real diamonds.
I found an old letter from my grandfather.	You were wearing the same clothes you are now.
My dog had puppies.	We thought it was a male.
your own idea:	

2 Conversation building

Read the conversation out loud with a partner.
Change roles and read the conversation again.

Try the conversation again. Use new words from the Vocabulary Preview list.
Now make a new conversation. Use your own ideas.

Grammar Awareness *The missing ring*

Look at the picture. What do you think is happening?

1 Understanding
Someone stole Laura's ring. Listen to the police officer asking people about what happened. Complete the table.

Name	he/she was doing	Witness
1. Nick	....	....
2. Julie	....	....
3.	*swimming in the water*	....
4. Ken	....	....
5.	*getting some ice cream*	....

Someone is lying. Who do you think it is?
How do you know?

2 Noticing
Try to complete these sentences. Then listen again and check.

1. Nick .... a ball around by himself.
2. .... something cold to eat.
3. Jordan .... with Laura and watching ....
4. .... on the rocks.
5. Melissa .... some ice cream with ....

Now complete the sentence about who stole the ring:

Laura .... in the water when .... her ring.

3 Try it
Complete this question. Then answer it.
What were you doing when .... ?

> **Grammar Corner**
> *I was eating an ice cream when someone stole the ring.*

For Evidence Cards
go to page 103

Pair Interaction *Crime story*

1 You and your partner will create a crime story.

Step 1.
These are some of the characters. Decide their names, jobs, and nationalities.

Name:
Occupation:
Nationality:

Name:
Occupation:
Nationality:

Name:
Occupation:
Nationality:

Step 2.
Now tear out the "evidence cards"
on page 103.
Look at the evidence.

Imagine.
What is the crime? ....
When did it happen? ....
Where did it happen: ....

Every crime has a motive (reason).
What was the motive? ....
(example: to get money, to get revenge...)

Step 3.
Look at the evidence cards again.
Think of a story. You don't need to use all
the evidence. Or you can add other things
or characters.

Write an outline for your story. Don't write the
story, only list the main events.

Step 4.
Practice telling the story.

2 **Follow up**
Join another pair. Tell your story.
Listen to theirs. Which story do you like better?

**Don't make your
partner do all the work.**

Read And Respond *Mysteries*

1 Reading

Read this mystery novel blurb. What is the book about?
What do you think will happen?

A War Of The Heart
"Thrilling, a compelling read" - Boston Journal

THE PLACE
London and Berlin in the 1940s…loud, crowded beer halls and smoky pubs…tanks rolling through the streets…air raid sirens and people running for shelter…a world gone mad…and two people hopelessly in love.

THE PLAN
The enemy army was planning a decisive rocket attack into the heart of the allied forces in London. Everything depended on whether a top spy could pinpoint the location of Churchill's secret war room.

THE PLAYERS
Thomas Garland, Churchill's most trusted junior officer. He had a duty to his country but his world revolved around a beautiful woman…and Eva Dane, an agent for the enemy. But when it came time to sign her lover's death certificate, would her heart let her do it?

2 Try it

Write a blurb for a mystery novel.
Mention: the place, the plan, the players.

3 Shared writing

Work in a group of four.
Read each other's book blurbs.
Which is most imaginative?
Which novels would you like to read?

9 DIFFERENT GENERATIONS

- agreeing, disagreeing
- problems and complaints
- gerunds and infinitives

Warm Up *Changing interests*

Work with a partner. Write one thing that is important to someone who is:

1 year old ....

5 years old ....

10 years old *comic books* ....

15 years old ....

18 years old ....

21 years old ....

28 years old ....

35 years old ....

45 years old ....

65 years old ....

**Now join another pair. Read your list.
Listen to their ideas. How many were the same?**

Listening *"What are you planning to do?"*

Lynn Greene and her son, Jordan, are talking about the future.

1 ▸ Listening for key words
Listen. What things does Lynn mention? Put an L next to each one.
What things does Jordan mention? Put a J next to each one.

☐ It's important to make some plans.   ☐ I don't want to worry about money.

☐ This is the time to start.   ☐ I make enough to live on.

☐ I still have a lot of things...   ☐ I don't believe in saving for the future.

☐ It's good to be adventurous.   ☐ I do worry about you.

2 ▸ Listening for meaning
Listen again. What do Jordan and Lynn disagree about?

....

....

3 ▸ What do you think?
Who do you agree with more: Lynn or Jordan? Why?

 **Conversation Topic** *Generation gap*

Vocabulary preview

Which of these topics have you argued about with your parents? Make a check (✓).
Match each topic with a complaint.

Topics	Complaints
my friends	My ideas are too wild.
music	I should have a more conservative hairstyle.
clothes	I should wear better clothes.
my future plans	I should get a real job.
politics	My friends are strange.
my schedule	I stay out too late. / I should get up early.
my room	I shouldn't eat so much junk food.
my hair	I should stop listening to loud music.
the phone	I spend too much time on the phone.
TV	I should read more.
my diet	I should clean up my room.
your own idea:	
....	

2 Conversation building

Read the conversation out loud with a partner.
Change roles and read the conversation again.

Try the conversation again. Use new words from the Vocabulary Preview list.
Now make a new conversation. Use your own ideas.

Grammar Awareness *Dad, give me a break!*

Do you agree with these statements? Check the ones you agree with.

☐ Dressing well is a sign of success.
☐ Going to bed early is good for you.
☐ Borrowing money is unwise.
☐ Marrying young is best.

Do you think your parents agree with the statements?

1 Understanding

Listen to Laura and her father.
What does Laura's father want her to do?
List four things.

1. ....
2. ....
3. ....
4. ....

2 Noticing

Finish these sentences.
Then listen again and check your answers.

1. .... keeps you healthy.
2. .... makes the right impression.
3. .... is wise.
4. .... is the secret to a happy life.

3 Try it

Write two sentences about things in life you believe in strongly. Begin with an -ing word.

....

....

Grammar Corner
Changing jobs is risky.   *Marrying young* is best.

Pair Interaction *Parents and children*

1 Are you different from your parents? In what way?
Fill in the chart for "Me" and "My Parents." Write one or two words in each box.

Then exchange ideas with a partner. Ask questions about your partner's answers.
Fill in the chart for "My Partner" and "My Partner's Parents."

CATEGORY	Me	My Parents	My Partner	My Partner's Parents
Style (clothes, hair, etc.)				
Music				
Hobbies				
Dating				
Marriage				
Foreigners				
Roles of men and women				
Raising children				
your own idea:				

2 **Follow up**
Now look at the chart. In what ways are you similar to your parents?
In what ways is your partner similar to his or her parents?

-
-
-

I THINK MY PARENTS WOULD SAY... MAYBE THEY THINK...

Try to answer even if you're not sure.

Read And Respond *Dear future me...*

1 Reading

Read this letter that Jordan wrote to himself. Which ideas do you agree with?
Check (✓) them.

Dear Future Me,

When you read this letter in 20 years time, I hope you'll be able to say:

• You have appreciated your life. You took time to "smell the roses."
  You have been grateful for the simple things you've got.

• You didn't let money control your life. You didn't take a job just for
  the money. You listened to your heart and followed your dreams.

• You were honest in your relationships. You didn't hide your feelings.
  You tried to make your relationships become stronger through honesty.

• You let your children be what they're going to be. You didn't try to
  make them into imitations of yourself. You tried to find out what they
  wanted instead of telling them what you thought was right.

• You remembered that you were young and the spirit of youth is a
  wonderful thing to preserve.

Yours, Jordan

2 Try it

Write a letter to yourself 20 years in the future. Write about the ideas that you think
should guide the way you live.

3 Shared writing

Work in a group of four. Exchange letters and read what your partners wrote. Which
ideas do you think should guide your life?

Group Activity *Chain stories*

Work in groups of five.
Choose one of the "story starters" below.
One person reads the sentence.
Someone else adds the next sentence. Keep going as long as you can.

The night was dark and cold. I was alone in the house. Suddenly I heard…

I don't usually argue with my parents, but this was too much. They said…

I was so embarrassed. I was doing some shopping when…

Crack! "What was that?" I asked? "Maybe it was…

My grandfather smiled and said, "It hasn't always been like this, you know. Why, when I was your age…

Think of a different "story starter."

Learning Check

1 Grammar check

Julie is talking to her brother, Jordan. Fill in the correct form of each verb. Then listen to the conversation to check your answers.

Jordan: Julie, I'm worried.

Julie: What is it?

Jordan: Well, you know that party I went to last night?

Julie: Yeah. You ☐ ☐ ☐ (*go*) to a meeting, but you went to the party instead, right?

Jordan: Yeah. Anyway, I got a ride back with Nick. He ☐ ☐ (*drive*) pretty fast. When he ☐ ☐ (*pass*) a truck, he hit a street sign. He ☐ ☐ (*drive*) very safely.

Julie: Did you stop?

Jordan: Well, I know we ☐ ☐ ☐ (*stop*), but Nick said it was all right.

Julie: Oh, great! Not ☐ (*stop*) after an accident is breaking the law, you know.

Jordan: Yeah, I know.

Julie: So ☐ (*call*) the police now.

Jordan: But ☐ (*call*) the police now will get Nick into trouble.

Julie: Yeah, well, you've got a real problem.

What would you do if you were Jordan?

2 Vocabulary expansion - noun combinations

Match a word on the left with a word on the right to make a new word or phrase.

arm	ball
coffee	stand
dining	room
ear	lot
floor	star
ice cream	table
jewelry	box
movie	lamp
parking	ring
soccer	chair
tooth	paste

Can you think of more noun combinations?

....

....

....

....

Review Game *You ask too many questions!*

Work in groups of three. Put one book on the table.
One person (A) chooses a topic in a blue circle. A says a sentence about it.
Partners, how many questions can you ask about what A said?
You must touch the buzzer each time you ask a question.
Mark (卌) the questions you ask. Then someone else chooses a circle.

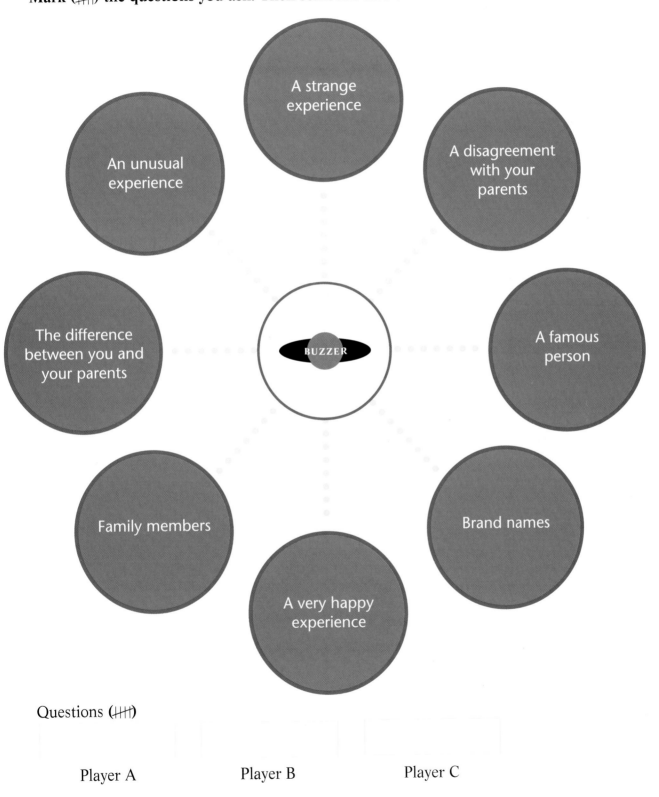

Questions (卌)

Player A   Player B   Player C

EXPANSION *Unit*

Learning Better *Think before using the dictionary*

1 **What do you usually do when you come to a new word in your first language?**

- **look it up in a dictionary**
- **guess the meaning and keep going**
- **ignore the word**

Dictionaries are useful. But sometimes we use them too much.
Sometimes you can <u>guess the meaning.</u>
Try to guess the words in italics (in English or in your first language).

1. Mary just went *idnesd fjureide* yesterday. She didn't buy anything.

2. Alex needed some pens and notebooks, so he went to the *fjirfkwedck djeri*.

3. My friends loved that movie but I was *fjeisjsiw* by it because it was so violent.

Now check. Did you write words with similar meanings?
1. window shopping (to look but not buy anything).
2. stationery store (a place that sells stationery: pens, pencils, papers, etc.)
3. disgusted (a strong feeling of dislike).

These are three ways to decide when to use a dictionary.
1. Guess the meaning.*You can look up the word later to be sure.*
2. Try the "baseball rule"- "three strikes" method..
   The first time you see or hear a new word, skip it (just continue).
   The second time you see or hear that word, make a guess.
   The third time you see or hear that word, if you still aren't sure, look it up.
3. Set a limit.
   When you're reading, decide you can look up only three words on a page. That way you have to decide if you really need to look something up.

Think about which ways will work for you.

---

2 **Learning better task**
This week, read something new in English.
Use your dictionary in one of the ways above (#1, 2, or 3).
Which way did you try when reading?
Was it successful? Did it help you read better?

74

10 WORKING WORLD

- wishes and hopes, advantages and disadvantages
- jobs
- conjunctions, complex sentences

Warm Up *Jobs*

Work with a partner.
How many jobs can you list in five minutes?
Write them.

Exciting jobs	Jobs that help people
•	•
•	•
•	•

Jobs that pay a lot of money	Jobs in which you meet a lot of people
•	•
•	•
•	•

Boring jobs	Good part-time jobs
•	•
•	•
•	•

Bad part-time jobs	Other jobs
•	•
•	•
•	•

Look at the jobs.
Which of these jobs would you like most?
Which would you like least?

Listening *"It's a great opportunity"*

Laura is talking to Jordan about a job offer.

1 Listening for key words
Listen. Check the words and phrases you hear.

- [ ] art gallery job
- [ ] in New York
- [ ] offering
- [ ] don't know what to do
- [ ] the manager
- [ ] a great position
- [ ] responsibility

- [ ] good pay
- [ ] do something you really want
- [ ] bad for your career
- [ ] have to move
- [ ] expensive to live
- [ ] see each other
- [ ] really miss you

2 Listening for meaning
Listen again. What are the good points of the job?
What are the bad points?

good points

bad points

3 What do you think?
Do you think Jordan wants Laura to accept the job?
How do you know?

Conversation Topic *New jobs*

Vocabulary preview

Look at each good point and bad point. Think of one job that fits each description.

Good Points	Jobs	Bad Points
You:		*You:*
meet a lot of famous people	sports announcer	have to travel all the time
earn lots of money	professional athlete	see a lot of suffering
might become famous	movie actor	lose your privacy
earn money listening to music	music critic	have to work at night
can work on movies you like	movie director	have trouble finding steady
can stay in shape easily	aerobics instructor	work
get to travel	ambulance driver	don't have much room for
help people	pop star	advancement
get to be creative	truck driver	have trouble making a
	musician	living
your own idea:	English teacher	

2 Conversation building

Read the conversation out loud with a partner.
Change roles and read the conversation again.

Try the conversation again. Use new words from the Vocabulary Preview list.
Now make a new conversation. Use your own ideas.

Grammar Awareness *Great hopes, small expectations*

What do you hope to be? What job would suit you best?

1 Understanding
Listen to Nick, Laura, Jordan and Julie. Complete the table.

	Desired job	Problem
Nick		
Laura		
Jordan		
Julie		

2 Noticing
Complete these sentences. Then listen again and check your answers.

1. You want to be a politician ....
2. You want to be a painter ....
3. .... , you want to be a teacher.
4. .... , you want to own your own business.

3 Try it
Complete this sentence about your future.

Even though .... , I'd like to be a ....

Grammar Corner
Even though it's hard to make a living, I'd like to be a painter.

For Job Cards
go to page 105

 Pair Interaction *What's my line?*

Work with a partner. You will think of a job and your partner will try to guess what it is.

Think of 10 yes/no questions to ask to find out the job.

Examples
Do you work alone?
Do you make a lot of money?
Is the job dangerous?

Tear out the job cards on page 105.
Shuffle the cards. Pick a card.
Your partner will ask yes/no questions
and try to guess the job on the card.

- fewer than six questions —> your partner gets a point
- six or more questions —> you get a point

WHAT DOES ____ MEAN?
HOW DO YOU SAY ____ IN ENGLISH?

If you need help, ask.

Score sheet: Number of questions

Round 1   Round 2   Round 3   Round 4

 Follow up
Choose three of the jobs. Tell your partner why you would like those jobs.

Read And Respond *I quit!*

1 Reading

Match the people with their letters of resignation.

college professor   *rock musician*   *law office assistant*

Which letter is the most formal? Which letter is the least formal?

Brad,

You'll hate me for this, but I've got to say it. You know I love being the drummer for The Pink, but it's not the same band it was when we started. A couple of years ago, I was as wild as you about the excitement and the crowds. The band was fresh and we were all young and a little bit crazy. But it's different for me now that I've got a family. I just can't live like this anymore. I have to get off the merry-go-round while there's still something left.

Phil

Dear Mr. Carpenter,

First, I'd like to say how much I've enjoyed working at Carpenter and Fisher law firm. I have learned a great deal and feel that I've made a solid contribution to the company.

However, I have decided to accept a new job with Stinson Art Gallery in New York. I will begin there on the first of next month.

Thank you for the opportunity of working with you.

Yours sincerely,

Laura Mendez

Laura Mendez

Dear Dr. Shaffer:

I regret to inform you that
I must resign from my position as
department head at the end of this year.

The recent budget cuts in our department
have made my job difficult to perform. With
limited financial resources, I am unable to
build the department that you and I agreed
was necessary. I can no longer carry out my
duties in good conscience.

Sincerely,

Helga Schmidt

Helga Schmidt, Ph.D.

---

2 Try it

Imagine that you have a job that you want to quit. Write a letter of resignation to your employer.

3 Shared writing

Work in a group of five. Show your letter to other members of your group.
Do they agree with your reason for quitting?

11 INFORMATION AGE

- reporting information
- opinions
- gerunds and infinitives

Warm Up *Media*

Work with a partner.
What forms of media do you use to get news and other information?
What do you use for entertainment?
List as many as you can.

radio

How often do you use each form of media?

Write **D** (daily), **W** (weekly) or **S** (sometimes) next to each type.

Listening *"I'm not sure I agree"*

Jordan and Nick are talking about TV programs.

▼1 Listening for key words
Listen. Check the words and phrases you hear.

- ☐ change the channel
- ☐ a good use of time
- ☐ so silly
- ☐ when I grew up
- ☐ American TV shows

- ☐ all over the world
- ☐ influence on other cultures
- ☐ take it so seriously
- ☐ just entertainment
- ☐ just stupid

▼2 Listening for meaning
Listen again. Which opinions are Jordan's? Which opinions are Nick's? Write J or N.

- ☐ Watching a lot of TV is a waste of time.
- ☐ Most TV shows are silly.
- ☐ Some TV shows are good.
- ☐ American TV influences other cultures.
- ☐ TV is just for entertainment.
- ☐ Watching TV is fun.

▼3 What do you think?
Who do you agree with more — Nick or Jordan?

Conversation Topic *New ideas*

1 Vocabulary preview

What do you think about each activity? Select one opinion for each activity.

Activities	Opinions
Home TV shopping	It's a good way to save money.
	It makes you spend too much money.
Sending mail through computers	It's a nice way to stay in touch.
	It's a lazy way to communicate.
Using a laptop computer in your car	It's a good way to save time.
	It's a terrible way to do your work.
Getting your news from the TV	It's the best way to find out what's going on.
	It's very superficial.
Teaching your language to other people	It's a good way to share our culture.
	It takes too much special training.
Using a dating service to find a partner	It's a sure way to meet somebody.
	It's a waste of time.

2 Conversation building

Read the conversation out loud with a partner.
Change roles and read the conversation again.

Try the conversation again. Use new words from the Vocabulary Preview list.
Now make a new conversation. Use your own ideas.

Grammar Awareness *Watching TV* 🔲

What are your opinions about TV?
Check the ideas below that you agree with.

☐ Watching TV is very relaxing.

☐ Watching TV all day long is boring.

☐ Watching game shows is senseless.

☐ Watching a horror movie late at night is thrilling.

☐ Watching soap operas is entertaining.

☐ Letting children watch violent programs is safe.

☐ Shopping from the TV is exciting.

▼1 Understanding

Listen to Lynn and Dave discussing their opinions about TV.
Write L or D next to the ideas above they agree with.

▼2 Noticing

Rewrite these sentences. Then listen again and check.

1. Watching TV is very relaxing.
   It's very relaxing to watch TV.

2. Watching TV all day long is boring.
   It's

3. Watching game shows is senseless.
   It's

4. Watching a horror movie late at night is thrilling.
   It's

5. Watching soap operas is entertaining.
   It's

6. Letting children watch violent programs is safe.
   It's

7. Shopping from the TV is fun.
   It's

▼3 Try it

What is your opinion about television? Write three sentences.

It's

> **Grammar Corner**
> *It's useless to watch* TV.
> *It's frightening to watch* horror movies.

Pair Interaction *In my opinion*

1 **What are your opinions about TV? Complete each sentence below.**
Think of one or two reasons for your opinion.

_____ is the most useful TV program.

Partner agrees? ☐ Yes ☐ No
Why?_____

_____ is the stupidest TV program.

Partner agrees? ☐ Yes ☐ No
Why?_____

_____ is the best TV news program.

Partner agrees? ☐ Yes ☐ No
Why?_____

_____ is the most exciting sport on TV.

Partner agrees? ☐ Yes ☐ No
Why?_____

_____ is the most boring TV sport.

Partner agrees? ☐ Yes ☐ No
Why?_____

_____ is the most interesting talk show on TV.

Partner agrees? ☐ Yes ☐ No
Why?_____

_____ is the best drama on TV.

Partner agrees? ☐ Yes ☐ No
Why?_____

_____ is the best comedy program on TV.

Partner agrees? ☐ Yes ☐ No
Why?_____

_____ is the dumbest quiz show on TV.

Partner agrees? ☐ Yes ☐ No
Why?_____

Write one more:

_____

Partner agrees? ☐ Yes ☐ No
Why?_____

Then ask your partner for his or her opinions.
Does your partner agree?
How many answers were the same?

2 **Follow up**
List your three favorite TV shows in order (1-2-3).
Stand up.   Talk to other students.
Find out how many people listed the same programs.

WHY DO YOU THINK SO?

Ask your partner's opinion.

Read And Respond *TV reviewer*

1 Reading
Read this review.
What are the three reasons that the show "33 Minutes" is so popular? Underline them.

☆ ☆ ☆ ONE OF THE BEST ☆ ☆ ☆

Nothing lasts forever, least of all programs on television. In fact, in the world of TV media a lifespan of three or four years is almost an eternity. In this light, the brilliant and often controversial THIRTY-THREE MINUTES stands out like a rare and precious gem.

So how do you explain success? How does a show whose format looks so simple—interviews!—last so long and attract so loyal a following? Luck? No, my friends. The word is quality.

THIRTY-THREE MINUTES has the best, most thoughtful interviews on television. They interview people we want to listen to about topics we care about.

The interviewers are seasoned reporters who ask clear questions that get to the heart of important issues like "Where does our tax money really go?" and "Why don't we take care of our homeless?"

After watching THIRTY-THREE MINUTES we feel that we've been there, that we actually know the people on the show, and that we've learned something important that we didn't know before. *This is quality TV.*

There's an old expression: "If it ain't broke, don't fix it." Somehow those responsible for THIRTY-THREE MINUTES learned this lesson and learned it well. They discovered that people will stay with you if your product is high-class. And it is.

2 Try it
Choose a TV program that has lasted a long time in your country. Write a review. What are the reasons for its success? What kinds of people watch it?

3 Shared writing
Show what you've written to a partner. Underline your partner's reasons. Do you agree? Can you think of other reasons?

12 MEMORIES

- explaining
- first time events
- passive verbs

Warm Up *Old things*

Think of a really old thing in your house.

Ideas

*picture, furniture, medal, jewelry, doll,
photograph, quilt, sword, tea cup*

Where did it come from?

Who did it belong to?

Is it important or special? Why?

**Draw a picture of the object.
Look at your partner's picture.
Find out as much as you can.**

Listening *"I didn't know that about you"*

Nick and Lynn are looking through some old things in Lynn's house.

▼1 Listening for key words
Listen. Check the words and phrases you hear.

- [ ] lots of old things
- [ ] favorite toy
- [ ] look at this
- [ ] an old uniform
- [ ] in the army
- [ ] in the service

- [ ] Jordan's father
- [ ] Jordan's grandfather
- [ ] old video camera
- [ ] old movie camera
- [ ] making home movies
- [ ] such a movie fan

▼2 Listening for meaning
Listen again. Who did these things belong to?

rabbit ....

uniform ....

camera ....

▼3 What do you think?
Why do you think Nick is interested in these old things?

🗣 Conversation Topic *First time* 📼

1 Vocabulary preview

How old were you the first time these events happened to you? Write your age next to five of the events. Then match each event with an "emotion" word.

Events		Emotions
...... traveled by yourself	...... felt that you were in danger	nervous
...... kissed a boy (girl)	...... lived away from home	happy
...... drank beer or wine	...... ate a hamburger or pizza	excited
...... had a best friend	...... earned some money	afraid
...... lost a friend	...... smoked a cigarette	disgusted
...... got a bad grade in school	...... stayed out past midnight	proud
...... told a lie	...... flew in a plane	sad
...... drove a car	Your own idea:	disappointed
	....	

2 Conversation building

Read the conversation out loud with a partner.
Change roles and read the conversation again.

Try the conversation again. Use new words from the Vocabulary Preview list.
Now make a new conversation. Use your own ideas.

Grammar Awareness *A new way of seeing*

What do you know about the history of the movies?

1 Understanding

David and Lynn are talking about the history of movies. Read these questions.
Then listen and write the answers.

1. What are the names of the two French brothers who first showed films in 1895?
   a. Lumiere brothers   b. Cinema brothers
2. What accompanied the early silent films?
   a. sound   b. music
3. What was the title of the first "talkie"?
   a. The Jazz Show   b. The Jazz Singer
4. Who starred in it?
   a. Al Jolson   b. Joe Allen
5. Where is the film capital of the world?
   a. London   b. Hollywood

2 Noticing

Complete these sentences with the correct verb forms.
Then listen to check.

1. Films .... n't .... by an American. (invent)
2. They .... first .... in 1895 by two French brothers. (demonstrate)
3. Early films .... by music. (accompany)
4. The first "talkie" .... "The Jazz Singer." (call)
5. It .... in 1927. (show)
6. Thousands of movie theaters .... all over the world. (build)
7. That's when the film industry .... really .... (create)
8. Hollywood .... as the film capital of the world. (establish)

How many did you get right?

3 Try it

Think of another invention. Write three sentences about its history.

....

....

....

Grammar Corner
Films <u>were</u> first <u>shown</u> in 1895.
Movies <u>were</u> not <u>invented</u> in the USA.
"The Jazz Singer" <u>was filmed</u> in Hollywood.

☺☺ Pair Interaction *I remember…*

Work with a partner. Look at these topics. Do you remember the first time you did these things? What do you remember about each event?

The first time you ate a new food you really liked	The first time you played a video game
The first time you kissed someone	The first time you ate American-style junk food
The first time you remember crying	The first sports team you were on
The first time you wore jewelry	The first time you were given a prize or won a contest
The first time you spoke English to someone	Your first day of school
Your first job	Your first night away from home
The first time you visited a far-away place	The first time you performed in front of a lot of people
The first time you got into trouble at school	Write one more
	....

Follow up
Think back about this class. What interesting or unusual things do you remember?

- ....
- ....
- ....

Compare your list with another pair.
Which of your memories are the same?

> SORRY, I DON'T REMEMBER.

If you can't remember, just say so.

91

Read And Respond *I still think about you a lot*

1 Reading
Read Jordan's message to Laura. Why is he writing to her?

> Laura Mendez @compu.com.70321.50433
received: Sun March 7 23:45   943 characters
sender: Jordan Greene @alt.net.muse

Dear Laura,

I'm feeling very nostalgic tonight. I haven't told you this yet, but I've decided to take a teaching job in Tokyo. I'm leaving tomorrow.

You know I took it pretty hard when you decided to move to New York. I'm sorry I haven't written or called to ask you about your new job – I guess I'm still so heartbroken. Since you've been gone, I realize how great it was being with you. I miss all the things we shared together – all of our long talks together, our hikes in the mountains, all that stuff.

I finally decided to do something different, to get away from here and get a new perspective on my life. But I just can't leave behind all our memories.

This letter is the last thing I'm doing before I pack up my computer, and I think it's important for me to say this to you: I still think about you a lot. I really do hope that we'll be able to meet again – in Tokyo, in New York, or somewhere.

Love,
Jordan

2 Try it
Write a nostalgic message to someone. Tell them about your memories.

3 Shared writing
Work in a group of four. Show your messages to members of your group. Which ones are similar?

Group Activity *Talking in circles*

You have learned a lot about English. Think about these questions:
- How do you like to study English?
- What don't you like to do?
- What helps you learn?
- What are you good at doing in English?
- In what ways do you need to improve?
- How can you use English more often outside of class?
- How can you use English after this class ends?

Work with a partner. Talk about learning English.
Try to speak for two minutes. Partner, don't talk. Just listen.
After two minutes, the partner asks questions.

Then change. The partner speaks for two minutes.

Change partners. Do the same thing.
This time, you can speak for only 90 seconds.
Try to say just as much.

This time, you have only 75 seconds.

Could you say the same amount in 75 seconds? ☐ yes ☐ almost ☐ no

Learning Check

1 Grammar check

Read the sentences. Six are correct. Six have mistakes.
If a sentence is correct, write OK. If a sentence has a mistake, correct it.

(bet)

1. Even though Nick is shy but he wants to be a teacher. ☐ OK?
2. A waste of time watching game shows. ☐ OK?
3. Films invented by two Frenchmen. ☐ OK?
4. Laura is not very patient but she wants to be a painter. ☐ OK?
5. It is thrilling to watch a horror movie. ☐ OK?
6. The first "talkie" was shown in 1927. ☐ OK?
7. Even though studied music for years, Julie did not become a musician. ☐ OK?
8. Shopping from the TV it is very exciting. ☐ OK?
9. Most early films was accompanying by music. ☐ OK?
10. Even though Laura loved Jordan, she decided to move to New York. ☐ OK?
11. It is boring to watch TV movies all day. ☐ OK?
12. Many cinemas were built in the 1940s. ☐ OK?

Grammar market

How sure are you? You have $1000 to bet. You must bet on six sentences.
How much will you bet on each sentence ($100 to $500)?

Now work in a group of four. Compare your answers. Decide which are correct.

- If you were wrong, you lose your "bet money" for that sentence.
- If you were correct, you win your "bet money" for that sentence.

Then check your answers with your teacher to be sure.
Who in your group "won" the most money?

2 Vocabulary expansion
Look at the underlined "conversational" words below.
Replace them with more "formal" words.

1. It's fun working with kids.
2. I work in the morning and have the rest of the day for classes and stuff.
3. A: I think watching TV is boring. B: No way!
4. It's all just junk on TV these days.
5. What a cute little dog.
6. That's a really stupid idea!
7. Wow! That's cool.
8. Hey, Julie. What's up?
9. A: Let's go out to a restaurant tonight. B: That sounds good.
10. I was hanging around downtown on Sunday.

Look back through the book. Can you find any more conversational words?

94

Review Game *Conversation topics*

Work in groups of three or four. Each person needs a space marker. Put it on the START space. Close your eyes. Touch the HOW MANY SPACES box with a pencil. Move that many spaces. Answer the question. Partners, ask any question about what the speaker said.

H	O	W		M	A	N	Y		S	P	A	C	E	S	?
1	3	2	2	3	1	3	3	2	1						
2	1	2	3	1	1	3	2	1	2						
1	3	2	3	1	1	2	3	2	1						
3	2	1	1	3	2	1	1	2	2						
1	3	2	3	1	3	2	1	3	2						
2	3	2	1	2	3	3	1	2	3						
1	3	2	2	3	1	3	3	2	1						

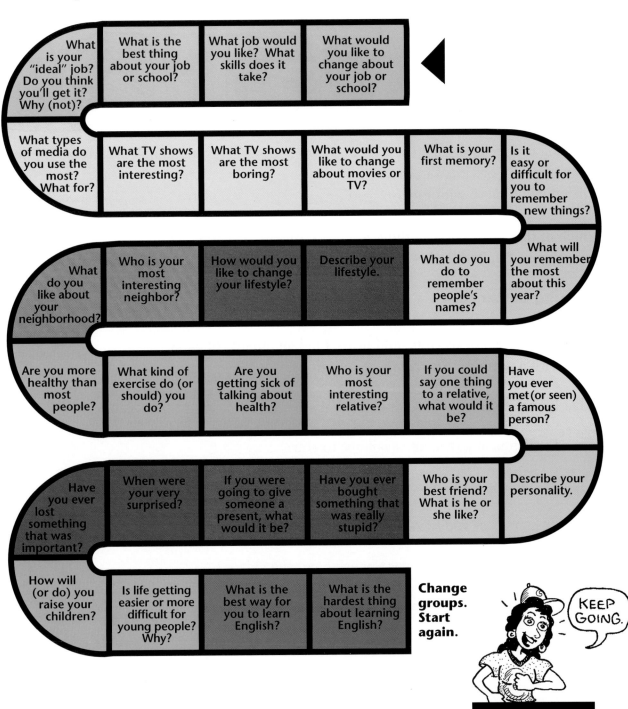

Change groups. Start again.

KEEP GOING.

You know how.

Learning Better *Use English or you'll lose it!*

This class is almost over. How can you practice English outside of class?

1 **Look at these pictures. How are these students using English outside of class?**

a. talking to friends in English
b. watching TV or videos in English
c. listening to music with English words

d. writing a notebook or journal in English
e. reading English newspapers and magazines
f. writing letters to English speaking people

Which of these ways do you think are most effective?
Rank them: 1st, 2nd, 3rd, 4th, 5th, 6th.

2 **Learning better task**
We hope you continue to look for ways to be a better learner after this class is over.
Think about ways of learning and using English outside of class.
Work with a partner. Answer these questions.

What libraries near you have English books?

What English newspapers are available to you?

What are the names of places you go to speak English?

What theaters near you show English language movies?

What video shops near you rent English language videos?

What bookstores sell good books and tapes for learning English?

What clubs or groups near you speak English?

The best of luck. Rod, Marc, Charlie, Greta, Jerome, and your teacher.

Pair Interaction *Planning a neighborhood*

Use these cards for the Pair Interaction activity on page 25.

Pair Interaction *Family history tic-tac-toe*

Play these tic-tac-toe games after you have finished the Pair Interaction game on page 35.

Dates

DATES	THE 1970s	THE 1960s
ABOUT 1985	AN IMPORTANT YEAR IN YOUR FAMILY	1988
ABOUT 100 YEARS AGO	LAST YEAR	IN THE EARLY 80s

Your relatives

GRANDMOTHER (FATHER'S MOTHER)	GRANDFATHER (FATHER'S FATHER)	A RELATIVE WHO OFTEN VISITS YOU
GRANDMOTHER (MOTHER'S MOTHER)	GRANDFATHER (MOTHER'S FATHER)	A RELATIVE WHO LIVES FAR AWAY
OLDEST LIVING RELATIVE	AN AUNT OR UNCLE	A RELATIVE YOU REALLY LIKE

Events in your life

GET MARRIED	FIRST HOME	FIRST JOB
FIRST SCHOOL	GRADUATE	LEAVE HOME
TRAVEL	DIFFICULT EXPERIENCE	FIRST FRIENDS

Pair Interaction *VIP party*

Use these cards for the Pair Interaction activity on page 41.

• a sports star name _____ Q1: Q2:	• a writer name _____ Q1: Q2:	• a business leader name _____ Q1: Q2:
• a TV or movie star (male) name _____ Q1: Q2:	• an artist name _____ Q1: Q2:	• a scientist or an inventor name _____ Q1: Q2:
• a TV or movie star (female) name _____ Q1: Q2:	• a teacher name _____ Q1: Q2:	• someone important in history name _____ Q1: Q2:
• a singer or a musician (female) name _____ Q1: Q2:	• a religous leader name _____ Q1: Q2:	• someone from fiction (a person from a book or movie who is not real) name _____ Q1: Q2:
• a singer or a musician (male) name _____ Q1: Q2:	• someone who is evil (very bad) name _____ Q1: Q2:	• someone you respect name _____ Q1: Q2:
• a political leader (male) name _____ Q1: Q2:	• a famous person from your country name _____ Q1: Q2:	• your own idea name _____ Q1: Q2:
• a political leader (female) name _____ Q1: Q2:	• a famous person from another country name _____ Q1: Q2:	• your own idea name _____ Q1: Q2:

Pair Interaction *Crime story*

Use these cards for the **Pair Interaction** activity on page **63**.

  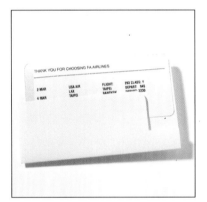

 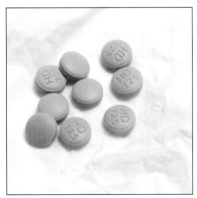

your own idea:

Pair Interaction *What's my line?*

Use these cards for the Pair Interaction activity on page 79.

 Tattoo artist

 Photographer

 Ambulance driver

 Athlete

 Movie actor

 Music critic

 Movie director

 Aerobics instructor

 Illustrator

 Pop star

 Truck driver

 Musician

 English teacher

 Pilot

 Mechanic

 Firefighter

 Video game programmer

 Composer

 Cook

 Snake charmer

Job Cards
For Unit 10, page 79

105

Appendix: Key Words and Expressions

Unit 1

LIFESTYLES
lifestyle topics
books
clothes
dating
family
free time
friends
jobs
money
sports
school

lifestyle ideas and activities
buy new clothes
cook
do things outdoors
do things with my family
do volunteer work
drive a car
eat in restaurants
exercise
get a job
get along with my parents
get home late in the evening
go on shopping trips
go shopping
graduate
hang around stores
like jazz
like peace and quiet
listen to music
meet friends
play on a sports team
read books and magazines
save money
spend money
stay at home
study a lot
study English
travel by train or bus
visit friends
watch TV
work hard
work long hours
write a lot of reports

Unit 2

PERSONAL HEALTH
health topics
alcohol
exercise
sleep
smoking
stress

activities related to health
argue with people
call a friend
do yoga
drink alcohol
eat a lot of red meat
eat healthy food
exercise outdoors
exercise regularly
get enough sleep
let go
listen to music
play video games
read a book
relax
see a movie
smoke cigarettes
take a nap
take crowded trains
take hot baths
take long walks
take my dog for a walk
work too hard
worry about things

Unit 3

LIVING SPACE
topics
messy apartments
neighbor problems
neighborhood plans
roommates

complaints
their dog barks late at night
their pets make a mess
they argue a lot
they don't return things they borrow
they don't say hello to you
they don't take care of their yard
they leave garbage outside
they make a lot of noise
they park their car in your
  parking space
they slam the door
they talk very loud

Unit 4

FAMILY HISTORY
expressions
(be) born in a different place
do the washing by hand
feel afraid
get married many years ago
go to work by bicycle
graduate from college
graduate from high school
have a difficult job
have kids
leave everything behind
live in a two-room apartment
move to another place
settle down
start a business
take a chance
work eight hours a day

Unit 5

IMPORTANT PEOPLE
topics
business leaders
a hero
a famous person
political leaders
religious leaders
scientists and inventors
singers and musicians
sports stars
teachers
TV or movie stars
writers and artists

terms related to personal
influences
dump someone
encourage you to read serious books
encourage you to try harder
find someone new
gave you a chance at a good job
gave you good advice
gave you your first real break
have a big influence
have more confidence
start in a new field (e.g. journalism)
take your life more seriously
try something new

Eric Clapton biography
alcoholic
basically happy
carry on with the blues

Cream
divorce
drug addict
Grammy awards
legendary rock bands
playing style
public spotlight
recover
rock and blues guitarist
series of concerts in Albert Hall
successful
versatile

Unit 6

PERSONALITY
preferences and actions

act cautious around new people
clean up all the time
feel confident
get up early on weekends
have a lot of parties at your house
have lots of ideas
have nothing to do
keep things to yourself
send birthday cards to all your
   friends
sleep late on weekends
spend a lot of time at the library
talk a lot
talk about new ideas
talk to new people
tell funny stories
think other (people) are better
   than you
think other (people) will laugh
   at you
try new things
try to answer questions in class
watch comedy TV shows
watch serious TV shows
worry about making mistakes

adjectives about personality

adventurous
aggressive
ambitious
boring
bright
careful
chatty
competitive
confident
conservative
creative
delicate
earthy
easy-going

energetic
entertaining
fiery
free-spirited
funny
gentle
honest
interesting
intriguing
neat
open
outgoing
playful
quiet
reserved
self-centered
serious
sociable
stimulating
studious
talkative
thoughtful
unusual
wild

other expressions

a jerk
an airhead

Unit 7

SHOPPING
topics

clothing
commercials
entertainment
food items
gifts
household items
personal care items
school items

items at stores

airline carry-on bag
alarm clock
appointment book
compact hair dryer
contact lenses
hair dryer
massage chair
pager
pocket tape recorder
suit
vitamins

reasons for needing things

being in a hurry in the morning
feeling out of energy
forgetting appointments
getting really tense

missing messages
oversleeping
thinking about my appearance
thinking of new ideas
traveling a lot
wanting to be more attractive
wanting to be more beautiful
wanting to be stronger
worrying about your first date

furniture

armchair
bed
bookshelf
chest of drawers
coffee table
desk
desk light
floor lamp
kitchen chair
kitchen table
potted plant
sofa

Unit 8

MYSTERIES
topics

crimes
mysteries
police investigations
unexpected events
unusual experiences

words and expressions

evidence
garage sale
motive
mystery stories
passports
plane ticket
police
present
rare postage stamp
real diamonds
rosebushes
run into someone

Unit 9

DIFFERENT GENERATIONS
topics

dating
hobbies
marriage
music
roles of men and women
styles

complaints from parents
being too adventurous
dressing too casually
eating too much junk food
having strange friends
having wild political ideas
listening to loud music
never saving any money
not being serious enough in school
not cleaning up your room
not dressing well
not having a conservative hair style
not having a real job
not having any plans
not marrying
not planning for your career
not reading enough
not wanting a steady job
not wearing nice clothes
spending too much time on the
   phone
staying out too late
wanting to travel around

Unit 10

WORKING WORLD
topics
advantages and disadvantages of jobs
changing jobs
exciting jobs

good and bad points of jobs
it has good pay
it's a great position
it's easy to stay in shape
it's expensive to live there
it's good for your career
the work isn't steady
there's not much room for
   advancement
you become famous
you can do something you really
   want
you can own your own business
you earn lots of money
you have to work at night
you lose privacy
you meet a lot of famous people
you see a lot of pain and suffering
you take on more responsibility
you travel all the time
you work on movies you like

jobs
aerobics instructor
ambulance driver
art gallery manager
composer
cook
English teacher

firefighter
mechanic
movie actor
movie director
music critic
painter
photographer
pilot
politician
pop star
professional athlete
snake charmer
sports announcer
tattoo artist
truck driver
video game programmer

Unit 11

INFORMATION AGE
topics
media
TV programs
TV broadcasting

activities
getting your news from the TV
sending mail through computers
shopping by home computer
teaching your language to other people
travelling to foreign countries
using a laptop computer in your car

expressions related to opinions
it costs too much money
it creates international understanding
it exaggerates everything
it saves time
it's a bunch of trash
it's a good way to (stay in touch)
it's a great way to save money
it's a sure way to (meet somebody)
it's a waste of time
it's all lies
it's an easy way to (communicate)
it's boring
it's dumb
it's entertaining
it's exciting
it's frightening
it's interesting
it's relaxing
it's rude
it's stupid
it's unwise
it's useful
there's so much violence

types of TV shows
drama
comedy program

news program
quiz show
talk show

Unit 12

MEMORIES
topics
early memories
emotions
films
personal items

events
being given a prize
being in a far-away place
being on a sport team
drinking beer or wine
driving a car
earning some money
eating a hamburger/pizza
eating American-style junk food
feeling that you were in danger
flying in a plane
getting a bad grade in school
getting into trouble at school
going abroad
having a best friend
kissing someone
living away from home
losing a friend
performing in front of a lot of people
playing a video game
seeing a movie
smoking a cigarette
spending a night away from home
staying out past midnight
telling a lie
travelling by yourself
wearing jewelry
winning a contest

emotions
afraid
disappointed
disgusted
excited
nervous
proud
sad
thrilled

film discussion
accompanied
early silent films
film capital of the world
first showed films
French brothers
starred in a film
"talkie"